YOU ARE

DOPE

OVIE SOKO

WITH LANRE BAKARE

Hardie Grant

QUADRILLE

Publishing Director Sarah Lavelle
Editor Harriet Webster
Head of Design Claire Rochford
Internal Design Katherine Keeble
Cover Design Jack Smyth
Head of Production Stephen Lang
Production Controller Katie Jarvis

Published in 2020 by Quadrille, an imprint
of Hardie Grant Publishing

Quadrille
52–54 Southwark Street
London SE1 1UN
quadrille.com

Cataloguing in Publication Data: a catalogue record
for this book is available from the British Library.

ISBN 978 1 78713 603 8

Printed in China

FSC
www.fsc.org
MIX
Paper from
responsible sources
FSC® C020056

DEDICATED TO THE MAN
UPSTAIRS: GOTTA THANK
GOD FOR THIS JOURNEY I'VE
BEEN ON SO FAR IN LIFE.
I'M LOOKING FORWARD TO
WHAT'S TO COME.

IN SHORT:

YOUR PATH TO DOPENESS WILL BE EASIER.

INTRODUCTION

Welcome to *You Are Dope*. Thank you for buying this book and investing in yourself. That's what this is all about – you. I'll be writing about my experiences and sharing some anecdotes and advice, but ultimately, this is about your journey. So well done on backing yourself and starting out on this path. We'll be doing this thing together.

The reason why I wanted to write this book is that I've been through a lot in my life so far. I'm still facing challenges now and continue to be pushed and pulled by life and the people around me – just like you. Although my particular journey is unique to me, the things I've learned are universal and it's important to draw from each other's experiences. That's what the people who achieve the most in life do – they mine other people's lives and experiences for shortcuts to improve their own. It's like their own personal cheat code for the video game of life. They tap it in and they level up.

This sort of cumulative experience will allow you to do so much more, partly by listening to the wisdom of others, but in some cases realising the missteps that our predecessors have made. It can allow you to skip some of the harder parts of life, not feel alienated by previous battles you've had to fight through or, at least, feel better prepared to face the challenges that can derail things for a lot of people, you and me included. This book brings together some of my life experiences coupled with advice I learned the hard way, so hopefully you won't have to. It's not as if you'll read this book and never make another mistake, but perhaps the next time you face a similar situation, you'll have it as a reference to help you navigate the problem.

In short: YOUR PATH TO DOPENESS WILL BE EASIER.

You Are Dope sums up 15 years of hard knocks and amazing moments. It's been a long journey and it's by no means done yet. Although born in the UK, I've lived and worked in the US, Greece, Spain and France, and have been on reality TV, becoming a media star in the process. I've faced challenges that have repeatedly come up in those various situations and surroundings. I've faced battles with my own mental health, my own culture and finding my place in life. I've got a lot to say, and you can read, understand and, hopefully, take some inspiration from it.

YOUR OWN UNIQUE PATH

You need to remember that you are a unique individual with your own set path. You are the master of your own destiny. You decide how to play the game and which route to take. However, there are many things that can crop up along the way that can mess with your navigation system. This book will give you a few prompts on how to recognise when you're potentially choosing the wrong path or making a bad decision, what to do when that happens, and ultimately how to fix it to remain true to yourself.

Trust me, when you stop being guided by that inner compass and start being led astray, the repercussions can be huge. For me it meant some really dark times in my life and many wasted months trying to be someone I did not want to be, acting in ways that were not good for me. Listening to and trusting your gut feeling is the most essential lesson in this book because that intuition, that natural beacon that is always operating within you, will take you to the right place – you've just got to learn to tune it in, and dial out on all the background noise.

WHAT IS DOPENESS?

Dopeness in the popular imagination is something that is not only desirable but inherently cool. It just *is*. It's hard to articulate it, but you look at something or someone who is dope and they just *are*.

DOPENESS IS INNATE, AND IT'S IN EVERYONE.

THE INNER COMPASS

You know where you are
right now, but where do
you want to be?

Look deep inside yourself and write down your personal goals.

_____

_____

_____

_____

_____

_____

_____

Now, what steps do you need to take to start walking the path towards your destination?

_____

_____

_____

_____

_____

_____

_____

_____

There are no boundaries on the word dope, it's not just one thing. There are so many ways it can be interpreted and that's what we are as human beings: individual and limitless. You could stand me next to ten different people and we'd all be dope, in very different and distinct ways. There could be a mother, working hard for her family, without the resources or money that many people take for granted. It might be a frontline health worker giving their love, skill and compassion to save lives. It might be a young person just being themselves, full of energy and enthusiasm.

In today's world, social media and TV portray dopeness as only existing inside some pretty narrow parameters: looks, money and your presence online. That's nonsense. That just shows you the way dopeness has been commodified, and sold back to us as a product.

Dopeness is innate, and it's in everyone.

Remember: dopeness is not a product, and it is available to all of us.

You've probably been dope for a lot of your life and didn't even realise it. Remember the time you did the washing-up for your mum and dad without them even asking? Dope. Remember calling your friend and patching things up with them after a fight even though it wasn't your fault in the first place? Also dope. What about the time you decided to dive into something you were interested in even though you thought people might make fun of you? Hugely dope. Remember, taking a calculated risk (even when you think it might be embarrassing) in order to help others or chase your dreams is DOPE.

When you start trying to relate to the picture of dopeness presented to us on Instagram, for instance, you think 'hang on, I'm not like that'. It makes you feel strange because you can't relate to the perfect picture. In reality, no one can. I can't. You can't. It's impossible. How can you be as dope as the person with 600,000 followers and a load of sponsorships and endorsements? It isn't going to happen. I'll let you in on a secret: that doesn't matter. You're thinking about it in the wrong way if you're trying to emulate those people. And dopeness isn't just something that can be sold, it's right there in front of you and inside you. We need to change the way we think about dopeness as being something that can be bought, traded or purchased and instead think of it as something that can be nurtured or emphasised. It's something we all possess, that we alone control – not some advert on social media or on a billboard.

And what are you really seeing in that Instagram post? Certainly not reality. Social media is just a story, and the 'perfect lives' that you see played out in front of you are just carefully curated and specifically chosen snapshots of one single moment in an influencer's entire life. You have no idea about the reality of that person's internal state of happiness and self-fulfilment. So, when you try to recreate these moments in your own life, you're trying to emulate something that has no basis in reality, no meaning. We can't allow false pictures of perfection to affect our internal peace and the joy we're guaranteed to find if we follow our own dreams. You have to embrace what makes YOU special, not what you think should make you special based on the pressures of social media.

In order to find your dopeness you need to be aware of situations and people who work against you as a person. That doesn't benefit you. Drop those friends that are bringing negativity to you, unfollow the people on social media who you have an unhealthy relationship with – better yet, maybe spend less time on social media all together (I've got a whole section on social media later in the book). There's going to be some discomfort in doing that. We're programmed to think that without these things we're missing out, that you won't make it or get everything out of life if you're not squeezing every last drop of 'excitement' or 'entertainment' from the online world. Think about that. When has the online world offered you anything as fulfilling as something in real life? I'm not talking about the dopamine hit of getting a lot of 'likes' on an Instagram post; I mean something tangible that didn't last for only a few minutes and actually changed your life for the better in some way?

Ultimately, chasing after the true freedom that dopeness gives you, the freedom that following your heart brings, can come at a price. People can

**DOPENESS
ISN'T JUST SOMETHING
THAT CAN BE SOLD,
IT'S RIGHT THERE
IN FRONT OF YOU
AND INSIDE YOU.**

misunderstand you or marginalise you because now you're not following the herd. You're doing something different and with purpose – that scares people, especially those who are looking to the picture-perfect world of social media and trying as hard as they can to attain something that is not even real. It's destined to be unsatisfying for them, and there you are, forging your own path and not listening to the cues given by Twitter or Instagram. That shakes people. They don't like it, but in friendship groups there are always going to be disagreements.

There is a freedom and liberation in the type of self-fulfilment that can only be achieved by following your heart. No matter what others think, you need to trust your intuition. This will naturally lead you to relationships that are based on true substance. Yes, the conventional road is easier – it's the one most people follow – but don't you want to see what might happen if you follow your dreams instead of others? This mindset is where dopeness begins.

If you do follow your own path, regardless of what anyone else is doing, and your friends see that, sometimes they might doubt you. 'What are you doing?' 'Do you think you're better than everyone else?' 'What's Ovie's problem?' It can distance you from loved ones in the most extreme circumstances, and later on I'll tell you about the times that has happened to me in my life. So going down that singular road that is plotted out just for you is going to be hard. You will doubt yourself, a lot. But be mindful. Pay attention to your inner compass – that will be aligned and you'll know you're on the right path.

Like I said before, to achieve dopeness we need to rethink what we mean by that word – who controls that interpretation and what it means to each one of us personally, setting out on our own separate and distinct mission.

EVERYONE'S JOURNEY IS DIFFERENT

Everyone's journey and personal goals are unique. You may look at friends around you and think, we're on this path together because it's leading us to the same place: that could be sharing similar professional goals, wanting a family or desiring to live in a popular area. But those are just points along our journey; they're not the ultimate destination, and sometimes you only realise this once you've hit one of these milestones. You might get enough money to buy that car, or that flat, or the house in the exact right area, but once you have it, you realise something is missing. You're not satisfied. Is that because you were not the driving force behind that desire?

Was that something you thought you wanted because everyone else does? I don't think this is some wildly radical view – it's common sense when you think about it – but with so much noise and interference being beamed into our lives every day, it's easy to get swept up in the consumerist world we're accustomed to. Then, before you know it, you're slogging away to achieve something that, really, you don't want. What it's important to realise is that the real destination in life is fulfilment and happiness. These aren't tangible things you can park in your driveway; they're emotional goals that will shape each person's life differently. Dopeness is an ongoing journey – and it's unique to everyone – it's something you work on throughout your life, continually listening to your heart and mind to ensure you're on the right path.

I'll talk more about this later, but for now I'll get into my story so I can show you the path I took, and how I learned to be guided by my inner compass. Let's get dope.

DOPENESS DETOX

Six steps to remove negativity from your life and find your own path:

1 **Beware negative energy** – There will be some people you are close to who have got caught up in a negative way of thinking. Distance yourself from them to create space for positive thinking.

2 **Create alone time** – It might only be five to ten minutes in the morning, but make sure the first thing you do every day is take time to reassess and set some goals. You're in charge of your own dopeness and you set the tone.

3 **Start keeping lists** – What are your goals? List-making can help you cut through the competing thoughts and focus on what you truly want. Maybe start with a gratitude list where you note down everything you're thankful for.

4 **Five-star standard** – A lot of the time we hold people around us to a higher standard than the one we expect from ourselves. That needs to change. Everything you do needs to be quality. You can start with just getting up, having a wash and brushing your teeth. Consult your list. Can you achieve everything on it? Dopeness comes from holding yourself accountable.

5 **Don't follow the herd** – You can't be happy by conforming. You can't play a role and achieve dopeness. Start to consider your habits and the conventions you follow. Are they things you agree with, or norms you conform to?

6 **Make the jump** – At some point on your dope journey you're going to have to make a leap of faith. You've got to take a chance, trust yourself and step off that cliff edge. It might be applying for a job, it might be asking that person out, but whatever it is you'll have to jump to achieve it.

SECTION

1

FAMILY

AND

SCHOOL

DAZE

To tell you about my journey I need to introduce you to my family. That's why I'm here: because my dope parents decided to have children. This book exists because of them, but I've got to tell you about my brother, who also guided me through some pretty difficult moments. Like all families, our relationships weren't always simple and straightforward, but they helped lay the foundations on which my own house of dopeness is built.

OK, so here's the starting line-up in the Soko House:

PAPA RAY
AKA DAD

Funny and laid-back, but he doesn't take any mess. Definitely thinks he is the boss of the house, my father Raymond.

MOMMA BEAR
AKA MUM

No-nonsense, God-fearing disciplinarian who provides for the family and can kick your ass when you step out of line. The real boss of the house, my mother.
PS. No one calls her Momma Bear. I just made that up.

GREAT RAYMOND
AKA RAYMOND JUNIOR
AKA MY BROTHER

Academic overachiever, sharp dresser, brainbox, three years older than me and the person I looked up to most as a kid, my big brother Raymond Junior.

MOTOROLA
AKA THE CLOWN
AKA OVIE

My nickname growing up was Motorola, given to me by my mum who said I never stopped talking. My dad introduced 'The Clown' because of my non-stop messing around. In my house I was at the bottom of the pile.

That's the family. We're all incredibly different in many ways, but we make a great unit because of these differences. These are the people who helped to dig the foundations that I'm built on, but as my nicknames suggest, I didn't always fit into the family system easily.

'WHAT'S OVIE DONE NOW?'

Growing up in North London, I have countless stories of getting into trouble. I couldn't seem to stay out of mischief in school. In the Nigerian culture big family gatherings are common, but even regardless of the size or the gathering – small or large – these occasions were a breeding ground for gossip, status anxiety and a chance to nosy into what was going on in everyone's life. I would often have to face the music in front of the whole extended family for my misbehaviour. Pretty early on I knew I was very different from everyone else in the family because I seemed to be in trouble the most.

BIG BROTHER

Many times I just wanted to be like my brother. He was the perfect child – he gave my parents no trouble, was really smart, had lots of friends and he dressed well, too. My big brother is someone I still look up to, someone I envied, and someone who ultimately acted as a guardian angel for me during the toughest times in my childhood.

As the youngest I think I was given some leeway growing up, but there were also some expectations that had already been built as a result of my brother being so successful. I think he had a bit of a tough ride because he was kind of moulded into exactly what would have been considered the ideal child. He was smart. Really smart. He also had many friends, and you didn't have to worry about him getting into trouble or doing anything silly. He handled business and was expected to look out for me, as a lot of older siblings are. As a result, responsibility was drilled into him more so than me and I ended up as more of a free spirit. The dynamic of my household was that my parents provided, they taught and showed us how to work hard, and that was ingrained in us. We were told from an early age that if you want something, you have to go out and graft for it. That's what we saw my parents doing every day, so we never questioned it.

WE WERE TOLD FROM AN EARLY AGE THAT YOU ARE ALWAYS SUPPOSED TO WORK HARD, AND IF YOU WANT SOMETHING, YOU HAVE TO GO OUT AND GRAFT FOR IT.

That hard-working, grafting lifestyle meant that as kids we took care of ourselves. My brother gave me responsibilities too; his instructions were pretty simple: take care of your own stuff and make sure you don't get me in trouble. 'Because if you mess up, I'm in trouble,' he would say. That wasn't going to wash.

Raymond Junior was the one who got into the best secondary school in the area by passing the notoriously difficult entry exams. I wouldn't have got past the first stage of those tests for selective school. My failure in comparison to my brother was compounded by the fact that everything is so open in a Nigerian household. As soon as my parents found out, so did the rest of the family.

Nigerians are vocal, and everyone knows your business: good and bad. We would meet once a month – aunts, uncles, cousins – to sit down and share faith and gossip. It would be at a different person's house each time and a judgment would always be made on who had been bad or good that month. When I failed to get into the school my parents wanted me to go to because I failed the admissions test, I could feel the eyes of my aunts and uncles on me, discussing my failure. It felt like I was the outsider; no one else was failing as much as I was. I can't remember a time when I was praised at these meetings, and although I eventually got into the school thanks to my brother getting a place, there was a real feeling of shame attached to it. The judgment of the family wasn't intentional, nor was it done with bad intent – it was just the nature of the culture. Often, when we feel judgement or pressure from loved ones, they've actually just got our best interests at heart and want us to achieve our full potential. At the time though, it was hard to not feel shaken up. My inner compass was unsure of where I was heading.

It was natural to ask my brother for advice, but I was the annoying little brother, the boy who couldn't get anything right. He always had my back, so I knew that if he was annoyed about something I had done, it was genuine – he was coming from a place of concern for me and the direction my life was heading. He was smart, he knew how to navigate the world better than I did and he was setting the best of examples, but even the blueprint he was laying out for me wasn't enough to keep me out of trouble in school. I really didn't want to disappoint him, and I think that respect came from the fact that I wanted to follow his example; I wanted to be like him.

I would often speak to my brother about my frustrations. If there was a teacher who didn't want to listen to me or would escalate the situation and try to get me disciplined, my brother was good at recognising the truth in the situation and backing me up when I was in the right. He could speak to the teacher and my parents to try and explain, playing the role of a middle man, helping me to be understood and talking to my parents and my teachers in a way that they could grasp.

Raymond Junior was like a guardian angel. **Everybody needs someone they can turn to, and I was lucky that for me that person was my brother.** The family criticism felt awful because I idolised my brother. It made it all the worse because the happiness that he brought at family gatherings, where he would be congratulated for his achievements, was at my expense. Everyone seeks validation at various points in their life, and this was one of those points for me, especially because I struggled academically at the time. But I was left feeling attacked and confused – emotions that we all experience when we feel like we're not 'enough'.

Something was missing – I wasn't able to bring my parents joy in the same way he was. That was one of the first times in my life that I suppressed a part of myself and decided that I was going to be more like my brother. He seemed to be loved so much more because of his academic achievements. People took pride in him, whereas I felt excluded and shamed. I was constantly made to feel as if, without my brother, I wouldn't have stood a chance, which in all honesty was true. I tried hard to change my personality to be more like him. But it didn't agree with me; I was still disruptive. My parents would get phone calls from the school about my behaviour in class and it set off an internal battle. I started to lose my way.

I remember asking my mum: why am I always in trouble? What is it about me that is so bad? But she didn't have an answer. She told me to pray, but I was asking a genuine question: why don't I fit in? That experience made me question whether or not I could fit into that world at all. Should I adapt and suppress certain feelings, expressions and self-belief? **We all crave acceptance by our parents, partners, peers – but at what price does that come?**

DO YOU EVER FEEL LIKE AN OUTSIDER?

Write down some key moments in your life when you've felt like you didn't fit in.

_____

_____

_____

_____

_____

_____

_____

_____

_____

_____

_____

Now ask yourself, why was I craving acceptance in those situations?

We should never sacrifice too much of ourselves just to fit in with others, but we *should* strive to better ourselves in line with our personal goals.

BROTHERLY LOVE

What I learned from my relationship with my brother is that it's important to be inspired by, but not empowered by, people who you find dope. They should inspire you to search out your own dopeness and inner strength. But someone else should never be your source of power, because it's impossible to draw dopeness from someone else. You need to embrace your own path rather than rely on another person to empower you to do so. Someone else can help point the way but they are not the destination themselves. When you try to follow the blueprint of someone else's life you will ultimately feel lost and lack the feeling of fulfilment that only your internal compass can lead you towards.

For a lot of us it's subconscious. In my brother I saw someone who was supremely confident and successful, and at times I tried to copy him in order to succeed, but I ended up lost, being someone who wasn't me. Be mindful of comparisons; I call them the thieves of joy. Comparing yourself to someone else can lead to imitation, and no one's dopeness can be imitated; it's unique. Don't put yourself at a disadvantage. Remember we are all different and you bring your own skill set and talent to the table.

IT'S IMPORTANT TO BE INSPIRED BY,

BUT NOT EMPOWERED BY, PEOPLE WHO YOU FIND DOPE.

SCHOOL DAZE

The first time I noticed I was different from everyone else was when I transferred to my new secondary school in Mill Hill. That was when it became glaringly obvious. For some reason I couldn't seem to get anything right. I was always going in a different direction from everyone else. I was now in an affluent area and mixing with kids from stable homes. At my previous school I'd known a lot of children who were products of dysfunctional families and lifestyles, and that felt normal then. It had been a huge primary school, with four or five classes per year, but my secondary was a tiny school, where everyone seemed to know everyone. Looking back on it now, I realise just how different those two worlds were.

I didn't have an issue with fitting in socially – people tended to look up to me and I made friends pretty easily at both schools. **My problems started when I began to realise I had a mind of my own.** It was a hard thing to come to grips with because being inquisitive generally got me into mischief – I always wanted to ask questions. In class, if something didn't make sense, I'd ask 'what's the point of this?'. That's not encouraged; it's seen as disruptive and time-wasting because I would openly question teachers, or just generally push the boundaries.

AN UPHILL ROAD

When I was going to school in Mill Hill, there was a street I would walk up called Uphill Road that was lined with mansions, like the British equivalent of the 'American Dream' houses you see in places like Orange County in California. I would walk up it repeatedly. There was a specific house that had huge pillars outside. I'd walk past and think, I wonder what it's like inside that house? For most kids there are places growing up where you fantasise about what life is like on the other side of the doors. That house was the epitome of what I felt I wanted to achieve.

I wanted to live big – or so I thought. It represented a target that, as a youth, I thought symbolised success. If you live in a place like that you'd made it, right? Your troubles would be over. There's no way things couldn't be happy inside such an opulent house. Do you reckon that's how I still think today? Can dopeness be achieved through material gain? Nope.

FRESH PRINCE OF MILL HILL

I remember being so excited to walk into school on my first day, I was so gassed. I had the fresh braids and my new Clarks Wallabees. I was trying to be like master Will when he rocks up at the school in *Fresh Prince of Bel-Air*. I remember thinking, I want to go into school and be seen. I never wanted to go anywhere and just blend in. I never saw myself as just being another number, which is ultimately why I think I ran into a lot of problems.

The school uniform at times felt like a jumpsuit. I couldn't wait for the dress-down days when I was able to wear my own clothes. I wore some terrible stuff: long T-shirts, baggy jeans – it was part-American, part-British. If I'm being honest, I must have looked a mess. But I stood out! I remember wearing a huge blue T-shirt that was so big, two of my classmates could fit inside. At that age I was influenced by a lot of American TV shows: *Fresh Prince of Bel-Air*, *Martin* (Lawrence), *Boyz n the Hood*. I was even watching *Kings of Comedy* in primary school and repeating the very grown-up jokes at school, which, now that I think about it, wasn't a good look.

Despite all these internal conflicts about not agreeing with the school system, I still understood that the teachers were just trying to run the lesson. And in the Nigerian culture, what the teacher said was always right and was golden. Everything was regimented. You got good grades, got your head down and then everything would work out. But I didn't see it like that. I used to think, this can't be the only way. 'Does this mean that if I don't succeed in this environment, I'll fail at life?' I felt like a fish trying to climb a tree – it didn't make sense.

HOW CAN I USE WHAT I HAVE?

At school there was a clear financial divide between me and a good majority of the other kids who attended the school. I was by no means poor, I was just a working-class kid surrounded by (what I saw as) rich kids. The kind of kids who lived on Uphill Road. When I came over to Mill Hill I saw that everyone else had a lot – and I wanted some of that.

I would get £2 pocket money every day for school and some students would get £5. I thought to myself, 'OK, how can I have new trainers, how can I keep up?'. I was entrepreneurial to the extent that I even set up a little business selling sweets at school. I would make sure I went with my parents while they went shopping so I could get an extra pack of Coca-Cola thrown in the trolley. Then I'd go to school and sell the cans for 50p each; I could leave school with twenty quid by the end of the week. I started saving up and then I would reinvest the money to buy more 'stock'. It was a sugar-coated form of capitalism and a way for me to have more of the stuff I thought I needed at the time: clothes, trainers, drip. I would constantly think: 'how can I use what I have?'.

My parents were working their butts off. I knew I couldn't just go to them for more money, so I'd devise little schemes and enterprises. I'd play Penny Up the Wall, which is a game where you flip a £1 coin or 50p and whoever gets it closest to the wall wins all the money. I was always thinking, 'OK, how can I generate money? I want to get money in a way that doesn't hurt anyone.'

Of course, this was gambling, and I started to get into trouble at school (I would even bring in cards to play poker). You weren't allowed to sell sweets and chocolates at school either, so my little empire began falling apart.

Now I can understand why the school was so down on it, but at the time I thought, 'Well, I'm not taking anyone's money unfairly, they're getting cookies or sweets, I'm getting paid. Supply and demand, sir. What's the big deal?' The answer was: that's just not allowed. At the time I felt like I was disadvantaged by not having as much money as my friends, and so if I could use my ability and charisma to sell sweets, then why not? Why is it that only certain skills are allowed to push forward?

This annoyed me a lot and it made me rebel in certain ways because I couldn't agree with it; it felt unfair. Maybe it still is. I don't look back at that period and think I was an out-of-control young man who needed to be reined in. I was a kid from a working-class background put into a prosperous setting, and I did what I thought I had to do to fit in. My view was that, until you can show me or explain why this is wrong, or at least give me an argument that makes sense, I can't get behind it.

CULTURE CLASH

One of the toughest things for me growing up was that, at times, I felt trapped by various aspects of my culture, whether that was my Nigerian heritage, the youth culture I was a part of, or the British way of life in the neighbourhood I grew up in. I'm not for one minute saying I wish my upbringing had been different – far from it. The values instilled in me were vital. While I'm grateful for the values and unique qualities that my culture and parents gave me, I felt like the limits of this culture also backed me into a corner, which was a tough situation to be in. Eventually, **I didn't know whether being myself would result in success** in the eyes of my culture. That's a scary place to be in when you don't know whether your genuine thoughts, your genuine feelings, your genuine outlook on things are good enough to be accepted. So much of the time we battle with ourselves but we never vocalise our internal issues.

In the end I felt trapped by my culture at home and the things that society around me valued. The main mantra was, you need a good education, so you can get a good job, because if you don't you're gonna work in McDonald's all your life. That still doesn't make that much sense to me, considering McDonald's has an annual revenue of around $21 billion. That's not too shabby. But I didn't know at the time that it's OK to disagree with things sometimes. And I only found that out once I left home. Up until I moved away I didn't know if it was OK for me to think differently from the culture I'd grown up surrounded by.

Every time I did things differently or outside of the norm of the culture I was growing up in, it made me feel guilty because I saw it as 'wrong'. Because that's all I ever knew. That's what I thought was correct. There was this idea that you have to get good grades, and you have to study in order to become a doctor, or a lawyer, or a professional – that was the standard. That attitude would question the validity of basketball as a career. 'That's a game; it's not serious,' people around me would say when I mentioned my interest in basketball. 'You have to be serious in life.' But I would think, why do you have to be so serious in life? It is supposed to be enjoyed and cherished and loved.

There are many tenets of my upbringing – for example, ideas about respect – that I've hung onto to this day. But then there are also certain things about respecting your elders blindly that I don't agree with – that whole notion of 'do what I say, not what I do'. I did what my parents *did* – like them I've always worked very hard – and it's paid off. I saw the logic behind it. I watched them work hard and I saw that it moved them forward in life.

What I've now realised is that you can identify more with a different culture to that which you grew up in – and that's OK. I felt confined by the British youth culture I had grown up in – that was my normal – but once I left home and arrived in the US I immediately felt more at ease. I was suddenly surrounded by a culture that aligned more with my personal beliefs and goals.

You should never feel trapped or limited by the culture you've been allocated in your youth. Go out and find the type of culture and people that you connect with best and make them your new normal.

DO YOU HAVE A LOVE/HATE RELATIONSHIP WITH YOUR CULTURE?

Note down the things that are dope about it, and also those that are difficult.

_____

_____

_____

_____

_____

_____

_____

_____

_____

_____

_____

Choose what lessons to take with you and what lessons to leave behind on your journey to dopeness.

IT'S VITAL THAT YOUNG PEOPLE ARE ENCOURAGED AND GUIDED ABOUT HOW TO USE THAT INTUITION.

SEARCHING FOR ANSWERS: QUESTIONING CONFORMITY

The answers that my parents had to my questions came from their Nigerian upbringing, which did not feel that relevant in the UK in the late 1990s. Don't question your elders, don't question authority – do as I say. But I hadn't grown up in that. I grew up in a western democracy which my heritage butted up against. I couldn't get the answers at school, I wasn't getting the answers at home, so I was caught in the middle. Was I supposed to be listening to my intuition?

I think it's very hard for young people to come to terms with this situation. For me, it's vital that young people are encouraged and guided about how to use that intuition rather than told it should be ignored. What happens is that we start to tone down what that intuition says because all this time you've been told to suppress it. You can end up in a situation where you follow all the rules through school and university and then leave, and you're lost. You know how to navigate that particular world, but what happens when you step outside of that into a wider world that isn't necessarily governed by the same rules? You've been institutionalised and the magic trick has been completed.

If I was giving advice to my younger self, I would tell myself to **be aware of how to go about asking your questions, but keep asking, because you deserve an answer.** I believe everyone does. I believe asking these questions and learning more about personal and cultural environments can help us navigate our way using our unique internal compass. If it doesn't make sense to you, then it doesn't make sense – that's OK. Perhaps those answers will come later, but questioning conformity and culture is a genuine position. It's not just something troublemakers do.

ADVICE FOR MY YOUNGER SELF

1 **Awareness** – I'd tell young Ovie to be more aware. Be more in touch with the world around you and your impact on it. By being aware you can take control of your decisions and your life.

2 **Believe** – Self-belief is a crucial part of dopeness. At times I lacked the belief to truly push back and consistently head in that unique direction. I wish I could whisper in my ear and tell my younger self that I was on the right track.

3 **Keep asking questions** – You deserve answers. Growing up, there are so many conventions that make little sense, but if they're going to define your life, you at least deserve to hear the thinking behind them.

4 **But ask them in a respectful way** – I was abrupt and combative at school and with my parents. There's a way to ask questions respectfully which doesn't make it a battle – it's not a battle, it's a partnership. You're learning and it's OK to not have all the answers.

5 **It's OK to question your learned culture** – Culture should teach us about our history and values, but children shouldn't be bound by that. You can respect your culture, embrace it and achieve dopeness outside of the boundaries people try to set for you.

LEARNING FROM MY PARENTS

Even though I sometimes clashed with my parents, as I grew older they both taught me the importance of following your internal compass, in very different ways.

There are two things that stand out when I think about my father: his love for art and for music. He's an artist. Growing up in Tottenham, I remember him working away in his studio, which was in a shed at the bottom of our garden. He had a 9-to-5 job in the day, working as a housing officer for the council, and on a weekend he would work shifts as a security guard. But he lived for his art. He'd converted the shed by himself into a studio and he would spend hours and hours in there. He'd work a night shift and then have a little bit of sleep before going back out into the garden to continue working. My dad would be out there into the middle of the night and his music would be playing, loudly. My dad was a huge fan of Fela Kuti, but he also played blues, jazz and even a bit of Luther Vandross. Be in no doubt: he's very vibey, he's a vibey guy.

I thought he was fascinating. I always wanted to see what he was doing in the studio with all his paint and materials. My mum would come out and tell me off because it was time for bed. But even then I would sneak into my parents' room and try to see what was going on by peeking out of their window. I'd hear the jazz blaring and see the silhouette of my father working away.

It gave me an interest in creativity; **it gave me fearlessness** as well, because my dad was doing this thing that no one else's father was doing. My mates' dads weren't disappearing into a shed for hours at a time, listening to jazz and creating mixed-media paintings. It was unique, it was special. It also led to one of the most important conversations I've ever had. I remember him letting me into the studio and sitting me down on one of his paint cans. I can't have been older than seven or eight, and he told me never to listen to people who said I couldn't do something,

SOMETIMES
IF YOU DON'T WALK
DOWN THE PATH
THAT'S MEANT
FOR YOU,
IT CAN HURT.

to always back myself. 'Don't let anyone tell you that,' he would say. 'I listened to some of my friends when I was younger and I wished I hadn't.' He had studied art at college but didn't give it as much effort as he could have in order to make a success of it.

He told me that he kicked himself because he never went after art as a career. I had mixed feelings about this memory because, although it was encouraging, it was also painful to hear. Here was my father, a hard-working man who had supported his family but had something hanging over him: regret at not pursuing his passion. I could hear that regret in his voice. I could feel his pain almost. When someone who you look up to so much, and who was like a superhero to you growing up, is in that position, it hurts. To see how that had affected my dad... the conversation has stayed with me.

I think it shocked him as well. I don't know if he intended it to be a pivotal talk, but it was. He would remind me of his words from time to time: **'Don't let anyone tell you that you can't do something.'** One of the most recent times he mentioned it was during my time playing basketball in Spain, and he told me again to not let people tell me I can't achieve something I set out to do. After that there was a pause and he repeated, 'I really wish I hadn't listened to some of my silly friends growing up.' That was all he said; it was quick but the message hit home. He wasn't joking that time in the studio and he wasn't joking now. My dad is a fairly relaxed guy but he was deadly serious. 'Don't let anyone tell you that you can't do something' is a little mantra I've reached for many times when things have been challenging.

When I look at my dad's work I can see his passion. I see how dope it is. I see because my dad loves doing it. I see what he's done and it makes me think of what he could have done earlier in his life. It's a reminder that sometimes if you don't walk down the path that's meant for you, it can hurt. From a young age that instilled in me the thought that it would be tragic not to pursue the things I'm passionate about. It helped me dial into my inner compass and start to understand that we have these gifts, these passions that we need to explore to find our happiness. When I think back, those conversations seem like something from a movie, that pivotal scene where the father talks to the son and tries to offer him advice.

MY FATHER'S MESSAGE

To me, my father's story is a great example of why we each need to follow our inner compass. My dad's art is beautiful; it's an obvious gift. You look at the artwork and it's a visual representation of the beauty we all have in us. My father is lucky enough to be able to create these paintings through his gift, and I've seen the joy it has brought him and everyone around him. He drew a portrait of my mum back in the day. They've been together for over 30 years and I look at that picture and see the beauty in it, and also the potential that wasn't realised. That conversation with my father shaped my outlook, it made me realise that not doing something is always worse than trying and not succeeding.

Another of my favourite paintings of Dad's is a huge butterfly, which used to hang in the house. The butterfly is split in half: one half is really pretty with vibrant colours, but the other side is darker. It's a great metaphor for this book. The butterfly is a thing of beauty that you need to set free, but if you can't release it, then things can become dark; you can lose your way and you can lose hope, ultimately. I don't think my dad wanted that for me and that's why he repeated that conversation over the years.

If you choose not to follow your own path, then pain is unavoidable. It will come out in some way. Perhaps in anger, or sorrow, or even tears. That pain will pour out of you, and for me, hearing the pain in my dad's voice was a potent reminder to follow my dreams and try to make it in the world of basketball.

THE BOSS

My mum would always pronounce my name in one of three ways. The first was a standard 'Ovie' – no raised voice, no vowels or consonants elongated for effect – that meant she wanted me for something. The second was 'Ovvvvvvie', with a more pronounced 'v' which she drew out for a second or so, that meant I was in trouble. The final one was 'Ovvvvvie-aaaaay' – that's the proper Nigerian pronunciation and that meant I was screwed.

The way my mum called my name is typical of her: she showed me rather than telling me things. She's a boss. Hard-working, no-nonsense, fiercely protective of her family – she is an uncompromising but loving mother. We definitely clashed when I was growing up, but I had to respect how hard she was grafting. She was a property manager. She'd worked hard to get to that position but when she got there something wasn't right. When I was still in secondary school, my mother fell extremely ill, and we feared the possibility of losing her. It really brought us closer as a family and was one of the hardest periods of my life, but I think that was the same moment my mother came to the realisation that tomorrow is genuinely never promised. There is something about understanding your mortality that sends a jolt through your body and, regardless of whether your inner compass has been lying dormant for years, this realisation will wake that up.

Mum reached a point where she must have decided, 'This is not what I want to do.' She's always pushed us to work hard and stick to the plan, and here she was changing the script. My mum decided that she wanted to go back to school to study theology so she could go into preaching. That was her passion, that's what she wanted to do – it was what her inner compass was telling her to go for. I saw her, a woman who has worked tirelessly for her family, deciding to change career despite the fact it would have a financial impact on us all. It made me realise that regardless of where you are in your life, you could be the richest person

REGARDLESS OF HOW YOU THINK LIFE WILL WORK OUT,

WE ALL NEED TO ADAPT AND CHANGE WHEN THE TIME COMES.

on the planet, if you're not happy or following your compass, you will not be content. Only doing what is right for you will give your life true meaning and fulfilment.

At that time we'd moved house and I was in Mill Hill, where my friends were able to have all the flash new trainers and sportswear, but that wasn't an option for us – one of the reasons was my mum deciding to change her life and career. It wasn't what I wanted at the time, but looking back I can see how important it was for my mum. I was about 13 years old and I definitely felt the impact of that change, but the joy it brought and the happiness she was able to feel was crucial for my mum.

Looking back, I'm so proud of her. She showed me through her actions, not words. My mum made that huge shift and she's still happy doing it to this day. Her story showed me that regardless of how you think life will work out, we all need to adapt and change when the time comes. We might reach the top of a mountain we've been climbing, get up there and survey the valley below, only to think, 'This isn't what I wanted after all.' Perhaps that climb was just a way to get to your ultimate goal, which could be something that is dramatically different. It also reveals how there can be a price to be paid for searching for those goals. It could be financial, like it was with my family, but it could cost other things, like relationships or happiness, in the short term. Changes can reveal how we're meant to be on different paths from those around us; it can test our relationships, and sometimes push them to breaking point. My mum was brave: she had to be to make that change, and those of us who love her will always love her for following her heart.

DO YOU HAVE DREAMS THAT YOU'RE NOT PURSUING?

What obstacles are stopping you from following your heart?

_____

_____

_____

_____

_____

_____

_____

What do you need to do to overcome these obstacles?

_____

_____

_____

_____

_____

_____

_____

HANDLING PEER PRESSURE AND NAVIGATING MASCULINITY

A lot of young men struggle with the wider public's perception of masculinity.

It might be the clothes you wear, or the way you interact with someone you're attracted to, **but young men can feel pressure to conform to certain expectations that are set by friends and society.** This is something I have observed in men of all races, but it is amplified amongst young black men. It almost seems like there is a need to never back down from arguments – you can't appear soft and you can never show your emotions.

This constant pressure can build up and eventually manifest itself in various negative ways.

When I was in my final year of secondary school, the pressure to 'be the man', to be what society saw as masculine, to have money in my pocket (provided by any means), to look and dress a certain way, got me into some serious trouble that nearly stopped me being able to follow my dreams to become a professional basketball player. I, along with three friends, decided that on non-uniform day we were going to wait until the PE locker rooms in school were clear and then take what we wanted.

I'm not proud of it now, but at the time I thought, 'I don't have the means to get the things I want, so I've got to do something.' I couldn't afford the clothes I wanted. I couldn't have the freshest trainers. I wasn't allowed to sell sweets, and I wasn't allowed to gamble in school. So, I thought, I'm just going to take what I want. One of my friends had figured out that the PE teacher left a bunch of keys in his office which opened the locker room door. So the plan was, he'd swipe the keys, we'd wait until the coast was clear and then slip into the locker rooms, open up whichever lockers we fancied and take what we wanted.

WE RATIONALISE BEHAVIOUR WHICH DEEP DOWN WE KNOW IS COMPLETELY WRONG.

Before we went down, one of the guys said 'maybe this isn't a good idea', but I insisted. You don't back down; that's not what a man does. In my mind, at the time, a man was a provider. He was someone who got the job done by any means necessary; you made money because that's what women wanted and that's what society wants to see – those are the men who are praised and put on a pedestal, the men with money, they have the power. We went through with it, the class came back into the locker room and people realised a lot of things were missing.

The school did an investigation into what happened. The head of year called an emergency assembly. They discussed what went down and said that they were going to get to the bottom of it. At that point I felt terrible. I ignored it as much as I could. In my mind it was more important to be seen as this powerful figure. It was more important to be able to afford new clothes and a new phone. When I was questioned, I lied. I lied through my teeth.

We were all pushed along by peer pressure, the need to be 'the man', to do something which we knew was wrong but we thought would give us access to the acceptance that comes with the goods. I was hugely insecure, like many teenagers, but the way I masked that was by acting as if nothing bothered me. Would I not care that we were taking things from our peers and friends? No. Was I not worried that my parents would be ashamed and embarrassed of me messing up again? Of course not. That's what I said, because I felt the need to show that I was strong. I thought it proved I was hyper masculine and I didn't care about anything. That's what I considered to be important then, as a 15-year-old. I wanted to fit in and I'd do whatever, regardless of how reckless or hurtful, to fit in. I wasn't succeeding academically, but this was something I could control. That kind of rationale shows how twisted we can become because of the pressure young people, and young men in particular, feel. We rationalise behaviour which deep down we know is completely wrong.

At that point I was ignoring my compass. I'd got so confused by life that I thought by doing what we'd done, people would love me for the end product. I believed I was living the life that society valued. That's never the case, and if they love you for the end product, then it's the products that they are in love with, not you. It's hard for those who are older to empathise with young people who do things like we did, and part of that is because our value systems are completely different. At that time I did not see the world in the same way as my teachers or my parents did. I was trying to live up to an imagined standard, where having 'things' is of the highest importance. I genuinely thought that if I had these status symbols I would be valued and respected. If I possessed these things, then I would be loved and more popular. I was at an age where that seemed to be the most vital thing.

The school's investigation went on for three weeks and I thought we'd got away with it. Then I got a text from one of my friends who'd gone down to the locker room that day. He simply said: 'We've been caught.' I was sitting in my English lesson and a minute later there was a knock on the door, and I was taken to the headmaster's office. I was questioned and I continued to lie until one of the teachers lost it and started reeling off the evidence they had against me, including CCTV footage. They called my parents, which was terrible for them. I can't imagine what they were thinking. Ovie had done it again, although this time it was much more serious. I was suspended for 30 days and they would have kicked me out of the school if it hadn't been my GCSE year. That was the only reason why I wasn't permanently excluded.

In the aftermath my parents had a conversation with me. At that point they knew I wanted to go out to America to play basketball. They knew that was the direction my compass was pointing in, but they said they couldn't risk me going out there and something like this happening when I was over 3,000 miles away in Virginia. They said if I did go out there and messed up again, I could end up in prison, or something even more serious could happen. My parents said they didn't want to invest in me playing basketball if I was going to do dumb stuff like what went down at school. It was make or break.

THERE'S NO NEED TO IMPRESS SOMEONE BY NOT BEING YOURSELF

At that point I sat down with myself and thought, this isn't worth it. Why am I trying to be someone I'm not in order to impress other people, so I can get that ephemeral material wealth? I was risking losing one of the things I actually loved. Basketball was my passion (and you'll hear more about that in the next chapter) and it was offering me an opportunity to succeed. To risk almost having that taken away showed me how potentially serious peer pressure and the need to conform is.

I knew after the incident at school that I needed to change. **It was time to stop doing things to fit in.** I was good at basketball, I loved it and I almost lost the opportunity to play because I was trying to fit in with a group of guys and an image that was not me. I could see everything slipping through my fingers. I remember praying to God to give me another chance, I was that desperate. I told myself, if I get another shot I'm not going to mess it up because I'm pressured into doing something I know is wrong. I was determined to refocus and prioritise my basketball life. That was the ultimate goal, and getting caught up in bullshit was only going to stop that from being realised. I wouldn't have been able to live with myself if I'd ruined my journey and my life because I was trying to fit in with others.

My mum, brother, dad were all disappointed. I remember my brother sitting me down and saying, 'you really messed up there'. He explained to me how **there's no need to impress someone by not being yourself.** Anyone who you need to impress by not being yourself is someone you don't need around you in the first place. If you need to step out of who you are, then that's not a healthy relationship.

We all need those moments, hopefully not something as serious as what happened to me, but sometimes that shock to the system is the only thing that makes you realise you are heading way off track. Without that I genuinely don't know where I would be today. I was privileged to be able to learn that lesson so early in my life. It was dramatic and serious, and it shook me deeply. I learned through that experience that it was not worth losing who you are, and that what you have is way more valuable than anything else or any opinion than you can try to fit in with.

UNDER PRESSURE?

What do you currently do to conform to certain expectations that are set by friends and society?

_____

_____

_____

_____

_____

_____

_____

_____

_____

_____

_____

_____

_____

_____

Now ask yourself, why am I allowing myself to be shaped by peer pressure?

OVIE'S GUIDE TO POSITIVE MASCULINITY

1. DON'T IGNORE YOUR EMOTIONS

Don't ignore your emotions – don't reject a whole side of yourself because you think that's the masculine thing to do. That's nonsense. You can't bench press your way out of an emotional hole, you need to develop other ways to deal with the things that can send you down dark paths. It starts with reaching out to someone you trust: it might be a friend, a teacher, a brother or sister. Have that conversation. It won't necessarily solve everything but it will be the first step in tackling the things that are causing you problems in life.

2. NOTHING IS MORE MANLY THAN BEING ABLE TO WALK YOUR OWN PATH

That's what the strongest people on this planet do. They don't look for a path full of other people, they look for the path less travelled. It might not seem as safe but they're defining their own journey. To do that, you have to be comfortable and confident in exactly who you are.

3. KNOW YOU ARE WORTH IT

You need to feel you are worth it – that's what happened to me after the incident at school. Me and my friends were all guilty but we faced those consequences alone. None of them could help me with my basketball, that was on me. It was my future at stake. It was my dream that was going to be ruined, and at that point I started to realise I needed to invest in my own future. I didn't want to continue down that other path.

4. WHAT YOU HAVE INSIDE OF YOU IS ALL YOU NEED

As men, we can crave strength. You want to feel that you have power over your destiny, your surroundings, because when we're younger that's not always there. Walking your own path and tuning into that inner compass to discover what the passion is that drives you can be that source of strength. The outside world is just noise that you can choose to drown out.

5. QUESTION THE POPULAR OPINIONS THAT SURROUND YOU

Are you conforming to them without interrogating them? Do they stand up to scrutiny? Often when we're younger the things we believe are based on misconceptions – always take the time to ask questions and push back. You don't have to be aggressive but do it playfully – it's hard to do at first, but once you get into the habit of questioning conventions, it's something you can apply throughout your life to find out whether or not you're following your compass or someone else's.

6. SHAPE YOUR FRIENDSHIP GROUP WISELY

Once you've started to question convention, ask yourself if your friends are. What motivates them? Are you all driven to succeed? Would they support your dreams? Who are you seeking approval from? I decided to cut off the people in my life who weren't helping, those who weren't on that same path as me. The environment you're in helps so much because if you're being pushed by your friendship group, everyone wins. Everyone grows. Everyone has a better chance to enhance their own dopeness.

MY ROLE MODELS

IAN WRIGHT

Ian Wright was so unique. He was just himself. He didn't care what people thought. Football was becoming more mainstream in the 90s, there were huge advertising campaigns, and Ian Wright could be part of that commercial world while being 100% himself. He was embraced because of it. He was a naughty guy as well, which when you're young catches your eye, but he was an incredible player who thrived by doing things differently. He had a gold tooth, he drove a nice car, but he was consistently one of the best strikers in the world. He'd managed to become a superstar while retaining what made him special, and as a young boy that appealed to me. He was loved by everyone. He was utterly dope.

THIERRY HENRY

Thierry Henry was so good he didn't have to say anything. He just seemed to float around the pitch making magic happen. If people tried to foul him and get him off his game, he would retain his calm dopeness. He had this supreme confidence in his own ability, and that fed into the rest of the team, and then everyone in the stadium. Every Arsenal fan thought we could win every game because of how confident he was. It made me see the power of calm confidence, of knowing that you've got the ability to win at whatever your game is in life. There's no way you can get that level of confidence from being a follower; that only comes from walking your own path.

DAD

I have so much respect for my dad. Some people might not understand it, but my dad was my biggest role model. I thought he was the coolest person on the planet. I wasn't that interested in what celebrities or pop stars were doing; for me seeing my dad be so creative while juggling work and a family blew me away. No one else's father was an artist. He'd disappear into his studio and reappear with original paintings he'd imagined and realised himself. He was so different. His work was outside of the norm and from a young age it made me see that being creative and doing something different could be rewarding and rewarded. That was so dope to me.

BROTHER

My brother was popular, and he was smart. He didn't get in trouble at school, but he was one of the cool kids and it all seemed so effortless. He worked hard and set that example for me, but he made it look easy. I couldn't focus, sit down and get the job done, but he could and it was something that amazed me. That ability to think clearly and to have the discipline to complete task after task with the knowledge it was building to a bigger overall goal was so dope to me. It still is. My dad and my brother are the greatest role models I've ever had.

WHO ARE YOUR ROLE MODELS?

Note down the key people in your life who inspire and support you. How do they encourage you to be dope?

1

2

3

4

5

INTRODUCTION

FAMILY AND SCHOOL DAZE

BASKETBALL

LOVE

HOW DO YOU ACHIEVE DOPENESS?

ACKNOWLEDGEMENTS

2

BASKET BALL

THROUGH ALL
OF THE NOISE,
IN THE MIDST OF ALL
OF THE CRITICISM
AND DOUBT,
THERE WAS SOMETHING
THAT WAS TELLING ME
I WAS RIGHT.

It all started on my 8th birthday.

A friend of my father's stopped by the house and brought me a present. At first glance I thought it was a football. Why wouldn't it be? It was a round object wrapped in paper, and to me that meant only one thing in a country that is obsessed with the sport, as I was at the time. I opened it only to find, to my disappointment, that it was an orange basketball.

I was raised to be a respectful child, so I hid my true feelings and just smiled politely and said thank you. But underneath the smile I wondered what I was going to do with it. I don't think I'd even held one before. The next day, even though I wasn't thrilled with my gift, I decided to take the ball into school. I only made it a few yards down the street before disaster struck: I bounced the ball off my foot and it rolled out into the middle of Great Cambridge Road, where the 144 double decker bus proceeded to squash the life out of it. That was the end of my short relationship with basketball, or so I thought.

A few years down the line, when I was about 12, and by the time we were living in Mill Hill, I encountered basketball again. But this time it was something different; I actually enjoyed it, and it wasn't long before I fell in love with the sport. This game that I'd once rejected now gave me something to channel all of my energy into. It was a niche pursuit: not many people in the UK followed it and to a lot of my friends in Mill Hill it was just an American sport that was a very distant second to football. The first local club I joined was in Barnet, but I would train with lots of different teams around London, which was really common because court time was always limited at your local facility. When I began to take the sport seriously I met with negativity from some. 'You could never make it to the NBA,' some people said; others doubted whether there was any future in it for me in the UK: 'The sport isn't even big here.' But I didn't care. Through all of the noise, in the midst of all of the criticism and doubt, there was something that was telling me I was right. **It was probably the most important lesson I ever learned: to trust in that inner compass.**

I felt like I'd discovered something special; something that was just for me. I was good at it too. Good enough that my parents agreed to let me go to a basketball camp the summer after my GCSEs. This camp was where I was first scouted by a private school in Virginia. After that, everything moved so quickly – I went from looking at colleges in London, to going to the US embassy to get a visa, in the space of a month. It was one of the first times I realised that just because everyone else does something, it doesn't mean you have to as well. Standing out is OK. Being different actually has its advantages.

When I got that first ball as a present on my 8th birthday, I thought, that's going to sit there and collect dust, but within a few years of hard work, I was in America playing basketball. For me, basketball provided that passport into a different world, and the opportunities that would come with it changed my life forever.

Following your passions is a theme you'll see repeatedly in my story. Basketball probably won't be yours, but there will be something in your life you can't live without. Something you want to try or explore and are being told not to. My advice is to identify it and to not be dissuaded from it; you never know where it might lead.

LISTENING TO THE VOICE INSIDE

A lot of the time we find ourselves in situations where we're doing things we don't agree with. We do and don't do certain things due to societal norms and programmed reactions to particular situations. This makes you question what you honestly feel in your heart is right. You worry that it is wrong, a fatal miscalculation.

It sets off an internal conflict inside of you that might start as a tiny little battle. But then as years go by, and as more of those conflicts build up, what started as worry can turn into a real deep sense of frustration that you don't quite understand, but that you know is there.

STANDING OUT IS OK.

BEING DIFFERENT ACTUALLY HAS ITS ADVANTAGES.

ONCE YOU START LISTENING TO YOURSELF INTERNALLY, IT GIVES YOU A SENSE OF FREEDOM

This can so easily turn into cynicism and a habit of seeing things in a negative light. And then you won't even know how you got to a place where, all of a sudden, you're no longer able to see the beauty of every day, because you've spent so much time fighting yourself internally. This silent frustration fills you up until it becomes your 'normal'.

Even though, with the benefit of hindsight, it's easy to spot, you can feel like you can't even put a damn finger on it. And that is such a difficult place to be. The way out of that is realising that you can listen to yourself, and once you start listening to yourself internally, it gives you a sense of freedom, peacefulness and happiness.

Think of it like starting a conversation with someone – but that someone is you. You need to listen to yourself first, then you're able to continue the conversation – and whether the person does or doesn't agree with you, you will start to feel connected. **Once you feel connected you can begin to accept yourself, which is what everyone ultimately craves.**

I wasn't quite able to find who I was at home. Just like it was for me, a change of location or attitude might be right for you. I couldn't quite step outside of that box and explore things in my mind, in my heart, that I instinctively felt were true to me. That changed when I went to Virginia.

DOING IT BIG

My whole thing in life was that I wanted to do it big. Once I started to play basketball in England, that became the only thing I wanted to do, and I wanted to succeed. That was the one area in my life where I constantly saw progression, and it felt like I could be myself fully. I went from never having dribbled a basketball to getting picked up to play in America within six years. It was rapid, it was natural, and it felt amazing. But I'd had to fight to be able to play basketball in the first place. I hadn't been performing well academically. My mother wanted me to go into IT, but I knew which direction I wanted to follow. I understood my parents' reluctance to encourage my basketball. You always hear stories of people getting injured and not making it. There were fears that this was folly, that it was insecure and a gamble. In a way it was, no one in my family was a professional athlete, there was no frame of reference, but something was telling me to carry on and see where it took me.

When I went out to the States, it was a chance for a fresh start; I had new responsibilities and I grew as a young person. I was 16 and I knew I had to carry myself a certain way because there was no one else out here with me. I had a host family but I was there as a guest. Yet from the first minute I knew I was in the right place. Virginia is a long way from Tottenham or Mill Hill, but it felt like a second home. I remember going to the first training session and killing it. Everything was in sync – I tried something, it worked. It felt like this was how it was supposed to be. I was playing freely, not doing anything particularly special but just feeling that the chains were off and I was able to do what I wanted to. I was all of a sudden in an environment where the idea of being a professional basketball player went from being niche and extremely out of the norm, to a dream and goal that was not only seen as very achievable, but it was a path many were on. Naturally, I felt more at home. This is the same with all of us in some sense, whatever your passion may be. When you start out, your path may be tough to follow, but if you obey your internal compass and continue in that direction, dedication and time will eventually align you with like-minded, similarly driven people who are walking the same path as you. Find your little community and you'll find acceptance and support.

Finally, I was proved right. I took a chance, against people's advice, and it worked out. I wasn't gloating with an 'I told you so' attitude, but I was content that I'd followed my instinct (and what made me happy) and it had been successful. Those moments are gratifying. Remember them when doubt creeps in and you question your own dopeness. It's those happy moments that you're working for.

MOVING TO VIRGINIA

When I arrived in the States I knew I still had a lot to learn. My family had given me all the tools I needed to thrive and had taught me as much as they could, and now it was time to learn from other schools of thought. I was embarking on a journey, piecing together different lessons and ways of thinking that I picked up from those around me. I had to understand for myself which of these lessons I should hold onto in order to better myself and my own unique goals, and which of those I didn't personally identify or agree with, and therefore needed to be discarded. This was an important step in my growth and is crucial for everyone. Life is a journey, and throughout it we have to learn to listen to the opinions and lessons of others, and then decide which of those lessons we are going to live by. This was my state of mind when I first arrived in the US. I think I had to leave home – **I had to go, start to open up and figure stuff out for myself to truly come into my own.**

I was so excited to be in Virginia and I loved it instantly because everyone was really warm. People would say hello to you on the street. Coming from London that felt strange. There was a natural distrust: what does this person want from me? But they were genuinely wishing you a good morning rather than trying to avoid eye contact on the Central Line during the 8:30am crush.

My first family in the US was completely different from my one back home. I came from Mum and Dad and my brother to a single-parent household. Miss S came from LA, South Central – Crenshaw, which was a neighbourhood made famous by *Boyz n the Hood* and N.W.A. She was self-made. She went into the military, she had travelled around the world and the first thing I noticed was that she had a big house and her son was driving a white Mercedes. I thought, 'Wow I'm going to have some fun out here.' It was the American way, the houses all with their own driveway, and a big backyard and loads of space. I even had my own room. It seemed mad to me. Sometimes new ideas and circumstances make you realise that there are things outside your culture and realm of experience that actually suit you. You fit into this new reality so perfectly that you almost start to feel as though you were born in the wrong place. It was ironic that I felt so at home, so far from my actual home.

The other thing that hit me straight away was that the pantry was filled from top to bottom. It was like the pantries you see on *MTV Cribs*: every snack you can think of, the fridge was full. In my house I was used to seeing a half-bottle of orange juice, a loaf of bread, some butter, maybe some stew and rice. I mean, like, real basic nutrition. But over here there are all these different meats, corn dogs, everything you could think of! In the garage there was another fridge that was filled with Gatorade and bottled water. I thought, 'Oh my god. This is nuts.'

The first thing on my mind was, 'OK, well, how the hell has she managed to do it?' What does she do? Is she doing something I don't know about? I was thrown. She was retired at that point and had obviously saved money; I was so impressed. When people have done well for themselves, in a way that we don't understand or doesn't seem conventional to us, it raises questions. Miss S seemed very happy to me, and it made me realise that success, happiness and fulfilment take on many different forms. People might question, or not understand, your path, but at the end of the day it's only your happiness and unique success that matters, whatever 'success' means to you personally.

The other big thing that hit me about the house was how Miss S was there for everything. For her kids but also for me as well. At first I found it extreme. She was there to pick me up every day from private school. She'd take me to training and then pick me up from training. Remember, I'm this self-sufficient kid from Tottenham whose parents haven't been to a single one of my games because they were out working. She would make a huge breakfast every morning. If I needed help with my homework, she was on it. She'd say: 'I spoke to your teacher, and I see you need some help with this and that. So make sure you can get a tutor.' I was just like, whaaaaaat? I was so used to handling my own thing. Part

I HAD TO GO, START TO OPEN UP AND FIGURE STUFF OUT FOR MYSELF TO TRULY COME INTO MY OWN.

SUCCESS, HAPPINESS AND FULFILMENT TAKE ON MANY DIFFERENT FORMS.

What does success mean to you?

_____

_____

_____

_____

_____

_____

_____

_____

_____

_____

_____

_____

_____

_____

_____

of me was like, damn, this is what I thought was on the other side of those doors I used to pass on Uphill Road back in London.

Every morning Miss S would make hash browns, eggs, sausage, bacon, and then she'd make a fried rice dish, and it would be ready on the table at 6am. She'd then make chicken for my packed lunch and tell me to grab whatever I wanted from the pantry, so I'd be grabbing Gatorade, taking Oreos. I could not understand this environment. It was insane. I'd take three Gatorades and a bottle of water... just in case. It showed me a totally different side to life.

THEY LEAVE THEIR BAGS ON THE FLOOR?

One minute I'm in Tottenham, then Mill Hill, and now I'm at a private school. The first thing I noticed when I got to the school was that the lockers were all open and there were bags all over the hallway. Everyone left their stuff out because these kids were so rich no one would steal from each other. I was, like, what the hell? What? This is insane. I've gone from selling sweets at school to going into the pantry and everything just being there.

So, I started to see the benefits of Miss S always being around. She was like Superwoman. It was wild to me and it really added another level to my respect of women; I'd seen how hard my mum worked and now I saw how strong Miss S was too. She was all about getting shit done.

I remember at Christmas, I wasn't used to getting lots of gifts – we'd get one main present, maybe a pair of trainers or a games console, and a chocolate calendar – but it wasn't a big production. But Miss S put a load of gifts under the tree and it was such a special day. Staying with them was the first step towards me beginning to back myself, having that unwavering, constant support which, back home, my parents weren't always able to give because they were working so hard.

In her home she was always of the mindset, 'Whatever you want to do, we'll figure it out.' That's what I saw with her. Her children were encouraged to do other things – her son loved lacrosse and ice skating, her daughter loved horse riding. They were given the license to explore things that they found interesting and exciting. The idea of being able to explore any interest or hobby you had was wild to me. With this freedom, and the support of those who care about them, children are able to grow up with the belief that they can be anything they want to be and achieve anything they set their mind to.

When you are surrounded by friends and family who share an encouraging and supportive opinion of who you are and what you do, it has a hugely positive impact on your confidence and self-belief. This is very important. Passing comments have probably killed the most dreams on this planet. I'm not talking about the people in your life who clearly don't have your best at heart – they're pretty easy to recognise and block out. It's the people who are inherently negative and fighting their own internal battles who you need to avoid. **You don't want to share an environment with someone whose internal frustration impacts negatively on your own confidence** – find a support system instead.

Negativity from those you love and care about – family, friends or mentors – can be most detrimental. Comments from family as I was growing up often backed me into a box, a cultural box, where the rules and parameters were rigid and limited. It could be as simple as someone saying, 'Nah, we don't do that, that's silly' when I suggested an activity that I wanted to try. It could be something as small and innocuous as that, which would plant a seed of doubt. Rather than being encouraged to explore my interests and potential, in the UK I often felt that I was being forced to revert and conform.

DOPE LESSON

Learn to counterattack doubt

So what's the answer? You have to become aware of self-doubt and counter-attack it immediately: in your mind, say 'Yes, I can do that.' We all have the little voice inside that speaks to each one of us. Don't let passing negative comments brainwash that positive voice in your head.

I believe everyone has their own truth that can't be denied, but your mind can be affected by everything else around you.

With my second family in the USA there was a lot of support. I saw that the children there were encouraged to do whatever they wanted to do. Seeing that was so liberating; I experienced a feeling of freedom simply being around these people, and taking on board and listening to encouragement. Something as simple as 'Yeah, we'll give a try' is the polar opposite of the negativity that can make you doubt yourself.

Those positive comments need to be what fills your mind. This will allow you to build and develop a mindset that affirms and focuses your gut feeling. You'll be able to act as yourself and act with peace, without frustration. You'll gain strength and belief in your own path without fear of backlash or negative opinions of others.

This was the journey that I went on in Virginia. Small, positive actions that I benefited and learned from – like how Miss S would not only be at all of her son's football matches, she'd be at all my basketball games too, and would then take her daughter to piano and horse-riding lessons. The house was dotted with pictures of them doing all of these things, they were constant reminders of what can be achieved when you say 'Yes, we're doing this.'

Are you in that environment at home, school or work? Do your friends encourage your pursuits? You need somewhere in your life where they are encouraged, it's an essential part of growth. We all need that safe space.

LEAVING THE SAFE SPACE

I was in this environment where I was growing in my own way. So why would I want to leave? I'd played well that junior year and had one university scholarship offer, but the standard in the public school system was higher. This was where the dogs were, the hungry kids. Those players who were fighting harder and playing the hardest. I saw one team in the public school system who were on another level. They played for the state title and it was on TV. I watched that game and the intensity level was like nothing I'd seen before. I thought: that's real. I knew then I couldn't comfortably stay where I was playing for another year, all the while knowing that the school I'd watched on TV was playing the highest level of basketball in the state – I would just be doing myself a disservice. I was on the right path when I first got to the US – playing basketball at a private school that had a 100% graduation rate with 100% of the students going on to university – but I quickly realised that I had to change my situation again in order to stay true to my goal of being a professional basketball player. I was comfortable where I was and could have easily stayed, but deep down I knew that none of the success I would achieve at private school would bring me the level of happiness and fulfilment that following my dreams would. I had to follow my internal compass, change lanes and change schools. The new school was called Bethel.

What made the move easier was the fact that I had been living with people who were so encouraging of what I wanted to do. Living in that environment builds up courage inside you. You're no longer afraid of the speed bumps or the transition period. You're no longer afraid of any growing pains because your mind is telling you to follow your gut. Your inner compass is telling you to keep on going in that direction.

That compass can lead us to the end of the rainbow or the promised land. But if your mind doesn't agree with it, it can sometimes have you going in the opposite direction. When you're going in the wrong direction, the compass starts to spin out of control – you don't know where north is, east becomes west and vice versa. It can leave you with an unbalanced feeling and you know you're not going to have any peace. I had peace with my decision because all the dials were aligned. I was able to make the call that I was OK: 'I just need to be there, that's why I have to go.'

WHAT I LEARNED FROM MISS S

1. COMMITMENT

You don't get anything without hard work and dedication to your task. I'd moved out to America and felt like I settled in quickly because I was in the right environment. Are you being encouraged? Do you have friends or family who are pushing you forward?

2. ENVIRONMENT

Being in or creating a nourishing environment is key. A tree can't grow without the right support, it needs the right soil and amount of water. We can't control all the elements in our surroundings, but we can figure out when our environment is not a positive one and make the brave call to change it.

3. SELFLESSNESS

Giving can be as rewarding as receiving. Supporting a loved one to reach their goals or grow and become the person they want to be is so important. By doing that we can give back. That is truly dope.

DOPE LESSON

The importance of a safe place

The biggest thing I learned from my time with Miss S was that her home was a safe space where I could develop. I couldn't understand it back then, but Miss S created a safe zone that allowed me to be free and grow into whatever I wanted. It was a space that allowed my mind to be creative. Being able to dream is one thing that we should all have the right do. Some people don't have this safe space, or haven't yet discovered it, but it's crucial to realise that you deserve to be in an environment where you're able to figure out your path and feel supported in walking it.

When you start hitting those bumps in the road, which are really just turbulence, it feels like it's fatal and that you're doing the wrong thing. But if you can get your mind to agree with your gut feeling, follow it and see where it goes. Because as long as that's all lining up, the bumps in the road home won't seem fatal. Having the space to sit with yourself and develop and hear your intuition more loudly allows us to learn how to trust ourselves and follow our path more confidently, in the knowledge that the initial fear of taking a leap of faith will pass.

It's like getting onto a rollercoaster and flipping out because of the first big drop, but it only lasts a couple of seconds. You're panicking like you're going to die when you know in a couple of seconds it will stop and everything will be alright.

Where is your safe space, and why?

_____

_____

_____

_____

_____

_____

_____

_____

_____

_____

_____

_____

_____

_____

_____

_____

_____

_____

_____

ARRIVING AT BETHEL

I pulled up to my new school. I had gone from a school where there were literally phones lying around to somewhere where your phone might disappear if you left it unattended. It wasn't a bad school, and the people were very nice, it was just a totally different environment. I walked past the toilets, noticing the missing tiles on the ceilings, the padlocks on lockers and the security guards patrolling the school. It was a crazy first impression. My first American school had been full of kids from the richest families in Virginia and the students were mostly white; now in this new public school, the kids were nearly all black. **I'd experienced the American class system first hand and saw how segregation still existed.**

Despite my first impressions, my inner compass told me I was in the right spot; I was where I needed to be. My inner compass was right, too. I went from having one division-three offer when I first got to the States, to having seven or eight division-one offers while I was at Bethel, which was an amazing achievement in one season. That whole decision process was a peaceful one, but it was only the fact that I'd been able to grow over the previous year, and received so much support for whatever I wanted to do, that allowed me to be in a position mentally where I could tell myself, 'Yeah, you can try it out.'

When I first spoke to Miss S about changing schools, she wasn't into it; she thought I was nuts. She asked me, 'Why would you go? You know everyone loves you here.' She didn't really agree with it, but it was the lessons she taught me that allowed me to make this decision. If it wasn't for her support and belief in me I would never have built up that mindset of positive thinking and trusting myself. She helped me change my life and I'll never forget it.

A NEW ATTITUDE

At Bethel there was not only the class difference, but the mindset – in this school it was about fitting in. It was a breeding ground for peer pressure, like most schools, but my experience was pretty different. I was an athlete so I was part of a different group – people gave me love.

I was the new kid from London. The questions they would ask, besides 'Do you speak French?', were things like 'Are there black people over there?'. I should have just told them there are only five – and you're meeting one of them. Other questions included 'What do you eat?'... It was real basic stuff, as if I was from another planet rather than just another country. They were lovely, but they didn't have a clue. But I was just happy to be there. Everyone was friendly and the initial shock wore off very quickly.

The difference between the attitude of the private school team and Bethel hit me when I went to a summer tournament with the high school team. I remember after one of the games, there was this little guy on the team who wanted to be the centre of attention. We started clashing about something. I was the new guy trying to fit in, and he was a freshman trying out for the varsity team – we were both in a similar situation. Like a lot of young guys, especially within our social groups, we felt like we had something to prove. We therefore ended up butting heads over something silly, something small, that simply made good entertainment for the rest of the team, rather than 'proving' anything to anyone. I decided, OK this guy is a little shit. And I felt like he probably thought the same about me. But then once we got to the dorm rooms I figured out I should probably bury the hatchet because we were teammates (and he was the only one who brought an Xbox). Everyone was in his room talking about girls and we reverted to being a group of lads playing Xbox and taking the piss out of each other. It ended up being a good trip, but I didn't forget about how we clashed as teammates. That was the dynamic on that team: you could clash and fight and scrap and it wasn't looked down on. A heated back and forth was seen as OK.

This fed into the game – we could clash, we could compete, we weren't messing around, people could go after each other – but once we went into battle against another team, we became a brotherhood because we were in the trenches together. Yeah, we've knocked each other's heads off just before the game, but that's OK. The mindset was, 'I can do that, because he's my brother. You can't do that to them. You're not one of us.' We all had each other's backs. We all learned our value to the team, and that was great, but what was more important was learning the value of ourselves. Once you've realised your own value you feel less like you've got something to prove to others. The more we became comfortable with ourselves and our abilities, the less we engaged in negative interactions. When you're fighting or taking the piss out of someone, you've got to ask yourself, 'What am I trying to prove?'. Confronting yourself and your worth, and fighting to be better, is much more constructive than fighting with others.

DOPE LESSON

Confrontation isn't always a bad thing

This one is tricky because constantly getting people's backs up does not work. You can easily drive a wedge between you and your friends or family, but being in an environment where there are certain standards which have to be met is incredible. It can be hard, of course, but bringing a professional, determined mindset to what you do is the difference between succeeding or failing.

IT'S TIME TO
CONFRONT YOURSELF

What are you trying to prove to <u>others</u>?

_____

_____

_____

_____

_____

_____

_____

What are you trying to prove to <u>yourself</u>?

_____

_____

_____

_____

_____

_____

_____

PEOPLE ARE FULL OF SURPRISES

I moved in with the coach, Coach Huck, when I moved to Bethel. I was sleeping on his couch, and, funnily enough, the next-door neighbour was the little shit I'd met at the camp – the one with the Xbox. We started playing basketball together out the back of his house and became friends pretty fast. He was called Dominique (Dom), and eventually he asked me to come and stay at his house. After a couple of weeks he asked me if I wanted to stay long-term. It was so generous and I couldn't really believe that the same guy I'd been going back and forth with in the tour van was now one of my best friends. He asked his mum and before I knew it she was fixing up a room for me to stay in. It was real southern hospitality.

DOPE LESSON

The people you clash with the most can become your closest allies

It makes no sense at first, but sometimes it takes someone real to recognise another real person. There's an initial tension that can evolve into the tightest of friendships. If you're getting that vibe off someone, don't rule them out automatically – my friendship with Dom changed my life.

DOM'S PARENTS

Dom's parents are two of the nicest people I've ever met in my life and they have a very unique relationship. They had a very different dynamic from the families I'd been with before: my own and Miss S's.

You couldn't separate them, they really did everything together. Dom's dad is very hard-working and his mum would work shorter hours because she had retired from the military. You could tell because she kept the house and all of us in order. Dom's mum had such a peaceful and calming energy about her. She would make sure that dinner was always ready, breakfast on the weekends was always a big thing, and Sunday was always church. There was constantly good energy around, so even now, when I need to clear my head and train mentally and physically, I go and spend a couple of weeks with them if I can.

Dom's dad grew up in Norfolk, Virginia, which is pretty rough. Very, very rough, actually. He had a tough upbringing and used to spar with Pernell Whitaker, who was considered one of the greatest defensive boxers of all time. Dom's dad was training for the Olympics but went blind in one eye from boxing, so he knew a lot about sport and about the ambition that comes with it – he knew what it was like to really want something. For him it was all about mindset. He was big on changing your mindset because, according to him, once your mind is in a certain place you're able to physically demand anything required of your body. For him it was simple: **mental strength is the key.**

DOPE LESSON

Any situation can become a positive

Dom's dad was very resilient. He was tough and understood that was a quality which would help him achieve what he wanted. If you're in a tough spot, if life isn't easy, in the long term that can give you something others around you don't have: drive. It can give you an edge, not just a physical one like for me or Dom's dad, but an intellectual one that makes you work harder, think clearer and be more inventive.

MY NEW LIFE WITH THE FAB FIVE

There was a group of five of us who spent a lot of time at the house. It was me, Dominique, Joe, DeShawn and Keyon. We all came from pretty different backgrounds but we were close. I remember coming back into Dom's house after playing basketball and Dom's dad would berate us for sweating over the couch. He was just playing around, but he was always engaging with us.

During these sessions he would break certain things down for us – his life lessons. He'd explain why who we hang around with was important. He'd talk to us very honestly and let us know why we shouldn't, or didn't need to, be doing certain things. It would be an open forum and everyone would feel free to share their opinions. If we had a falling out he would play the role of mediator, then Dom's mum would add her opinions.

I was amazed by the level of acceptance for everyone's opinions, these people from separate worlds. Even though the five of us were from completely varied backgrounds, with different kinds of personalities, Dom's parents were able to talk to us all and bring us into the varied conversations. It wasn't like at school, where asking a question was considered to be an insult; here it was welcomed and taken seriously.

I was so amazed because that was the first time I'd ever really encountered adults who were able to do that. I'd never met people before who were so able to connect and communicate with kids with such ease. I've thought a lot about what gave them that ability, and ultimately I think it came from his parents being so at ease with each other. They were so comfortable in their situation. I was in another safe space – one where there was no judgement, regardless of what was being discussed, so long as everyone was respectful and listened to others' opinions.

There was constant banter flying back and forth. Dom would hammer his dad for his dress sense. We'd say something funny about his clothes, and he'd always say, 'I don't know what you're talking about – I'm married.' As if being married meant he could wear whatever the hell he wanted, regardless of the fact that it made him look like he got dressed in the dark. It was always said in such a peaceful, playful way. I admired him because he was so comfortable in his own lane, his own uniqueness and his life. He was dope. For me, the way Dom's dad dressed embodied how confident and comfortable he was with himself, his life and his relationship with his wife. His classic look was a white T-shirt, shorts, then long white socks and some grandad sandals. He didn't care. His contentment is something I learned from.

Dom's parents were clear in their mind about their life, their journey and their priorities. I think this is ultimately what allowed them to communicate with all five of us so incredibly, without touching any internal nerves, and teach us all important life lessons, despite our different backgrounds.

DOPE LESSON

Never be afraid of a debate

You only really find out what you think about the world around you when you have your opinions interrogated by people you respect and trust. That's what my group of friends and Dom's parents were – that trusted sounding board where nothing was off limits. Can you do that with your friends? Are there still taboos? Do you never have your opinions tested? Test your friendship groups by questioning conventions – it's the fastest way of starting an argument, but it can also open up a healthier way to engage, one where your horizons are broadened by discussing the things that really matter.

LEARNING ABOUT LOVE

I think, for me, Dom's parents are the best example of a successful marriage. They have something that's very unique today because they are each other's best mates. They go travelling together. They enjoy just being in the house. That level of comfort and happiness was built from never getting caught up in what other people were doing. It's dope.

They are cool being in their own lane. That's where you're happiest because you're making progress and moving forward in a way that suits you. It's when your compass is confused and you don't know if you're making progress or not – that's when the problems start. I think a lot of people could learn from this; if people focus more on where their own compass has led them, rather than comparing their relationship to that of others and worrying what people might think, then they'll feel much happier and secure.

They showed me how the mind and compass could be synced up. As a couple they were very happy, individually and as a unit. I would learn a lot from the discussions we had. For example, Dom's dad broke down the spiritual implications behind sex, and explained about money and how if you're always chasing it, you'll never truly be happy. It was big stuff.

Just like at Miss S's, at Dom's I was able to grow with a family that allowed me mentally to believe in myself – whatever it was I wanted to do. That allowed me to grow. I had a family that showed and embraced their own happiness. They worked hard and they were able to enjoy life and encourage others to grow. Ultimately, **I started to understand how important it is to be happy in yourself because it affects how you're able to communicate with the world.** It affects how you're able to impact other people. It affects how you're able to help other people if they need assistance. The impact of not being happy in yourself and your path can be huge – it's the biggest obstacle to dopeness. I honestly believe that if Dom's parents were not in a place of internal peace and happiness in themselves, they would not have been able to have the impact on me that they did.

* * *

BREAKING 'THE SYSTEM'

After leaving Bethel, I started at college in Alabama. When I arrived, the coach wanted me to play a certain way which was very systematic. Things were black and white to him – if things weren't executed in a certain way, that was a failure, regardless of the actual outcome. He was an assistant coach under a guy called Bobby Knight, one of the most successful college basketball coaches of all time, who helped establish the Indiana system, which is one of the best in the world. He came from a tradition which is hard-nosed and no-nonsense: you did what he said or you didn't play.

Coming in, I thought I had my own ideas – I knew what I was capable of. But then I started to doubt myself and wasn't playing as well as I should. I couldn't be myself on the court with all these systematic rules in place. I ended up transferring after my third year because the coach got fired, but really I was stuck in a rut and losing my love of the game. I was playing a role that had been created for me by someone else and it wasn't sitting right with me. I used to dribble confidently and break guys down off the dribble. I used to be able to handle the ball really, really well. But I'd lost that and had almost become robotic. Now when I tried to do all these movements, I couldn't.

Sometimes you have to change your environment and start afresh, so that's what I did. I went to a school up in Pittsburgh where the coach was going to take the handcuffs off me. When you transfer schools you have to sit out a year and can't play. So there were a lot of nights spent shooting in the gym by myself. Hours of working on myself and trying to get back what I had lost. I couldn't even travel with the team, so I just went to school, did my classes and worked hard on myself. I remember being in the gym one night and it dawned on me – what had I been doing? Why have I not been backing myself? What is the point in me being out here? Then slowly the confidence comes back because you've known all along what you were supposed to be doing – I'd just been trapped playing a role, moving in someone else's lane, and now it was time to find myself again.

When I first spoke to the coach, I said, 'Look I want to play. I just want to be able to be myself.' It worked. At the conference (a basketball tournament) I led in points; I was on one of the all-conference teams and that was in the one year I played there. I went from 9.5 points per game on average to almost 20, which is a huge leap. That made me think, OK, I can trust myself again. I'd been so upset by how things had gone that

I'd started to question whether or not basketball was what I wanted to be doing. I'd been playing this role for so long that my perception of reality had become warped. I knew what my internal compass was saying, but I'd lost sight of the destination and it was hard to find my way back to the path. When making a change, you might be uncertain at times, but your breakthrough moment is just on the other side of those worries – you just have to stick with it.

COMING BACK STRONGER

Never forget: no matter how far off course you are, you can rediscover that sense of self.

I started playing against my new teammates in practice and I was killing it. It was so dope because I started to see that I found a higher level of

DOPE LESSON

Don't worry about turbulence

When there's some turbulence in your life, that's when people say, 'Look, I told you that you need to conform; get back in the box.' But when you're flying, you are going to hit that turbulence before you get to higher altitudes. You need to fight through that. Remember: it's only when you start questioning your ability that it doesn't translate and it doesn't quite work out. Turbulence is a part of every long-haul journey.

confidence, because I had gone through a difficult period. It's like battle scars. I'd been so down and not able to accept myself – but because I fought through it, it made me into a whole new animal. The focus was there, and now when people told me to conform, I was wiser. I was confident in what I was doing. I was more aggressive. I was determined not to go backwards. I wasn't scared to share my opinion, even with the coach. It shocked people at first, but when what you are saying makes sense, people listen.

It ruffled feathers, but those ruffled feathers quickly turned into respect. That's how it works. People see you've worked on yourself and gone your own way – people know, 'OK, we have to respect that', and acceptance, ultimately, is what everyone wants and searches for. **There's no better feeling than people respecting you for who you are.**

***

DOPE LESSON

Assertiveness is a tool in your quest for dopeness

Once you've worked on yourself, it will give you confidence in what you're doing. That assertive swagger. Not everyone can express that on a basketball court but everyone can practise assertiveness in their lives. It's easiest when you've done the hard work on yourself or studied hard for a test or a job interview and you know you're prepared. When you're challenged, you'll have the answers and the inner belief that you're heading down the right road.

NO MATTER HOW FAR OFF COURSE YOU ARE, YOU CAN REDISCOVER THAT SENSE OF SELF.

LEAVING AMERICA

As my time in America came to an end, I was offered the opportunity to work out with Golden State Warriors' D-league team, which is a feeder team that doesn't pay much compared to teams in Europe. If I performed well enough on that team, the idea was that I could move up after a season. But I wanted to come back to Europe and get some financial stability. My agent understood and began looking for a contract for me in Europe. An offer came up: Boulazac, a team in France. I wasn't sure – I knew that I would probably get a better offer if I waited, but I was also in a rush to start making money. I looked to my internal compass but couldn't figure out which direction I should take. Going to France didn't feel wrong, but it also didn't feel right. Ultimately, I decided that I had to try it, so I packed my bags and set off for rural France.

'WHAT'S A BOULAZAC?'

Boulazac is about two hours' drive inland from Bordeaux. It's not really a town or a city, it's like a big village. A lovely village, don't get me wrong – but I'm a London boy who had just spent five years in America and was now in a village where the population was around 6,000 people.

As soon as I arrived in France I felt like I was playing below the level I could have. The season started off well, but it started to die down midway through. There's a lot more about being a professional than simply playing. It's a lot of eating the right things, looking after your body and drilling into yourself the importance of consistency.

It was the beginning of a new chapter. In university you still have coaches and an athletic department that are accountable for you. If you misbehave there is someone else who will have to pay the price. Now it's all on you. If I'm late, it's on me. If I don't show up, I don't get paid. If I don't play well, I could lose my job. I'd gone from having not that much responsibility to having all of it. I did feel my childhood and time in the States had prepared me for it, but that was like practice; this was a proper game. The training wheels were off the bike.

I was also in a professional environment; this wasn't college. No one was dishing out high fives when you walked down the hallway; you were with people who were making a living and trying to keep their jobs in a high-pressure environment. It was the real world. You were also competing for that livelihood with other people: players who had families, children – real-world responsibilities. Here's this young kid, who can't speak the language and is trying to take their spot. It made the experience intense in a whole new way. The only people I could reach out to were basketball friends who were doing something similar in other European countries, but there were a lot of silences, lots of time for contemplation. I thought about the journey I'd taken and the choices I'd made. Would I act that way again? Did I need to change my approach to things? That was part of the reason the year was so up and down – there wasn't any consistency, and my inner compass was starting to waver again. Had I made a massive mistake?

DOPE LESSON

Finding solace in yourself

Away from basketball I'd started to have a lot of alone time. I'd had this incredible period of being in the States, growing up fast in a foreign country. Now, in rural France, the culture was completely different and I was a rookie on a team of seasoned pros. It was a big leap. But that time alone was important. I started to grow up and appreciate all the lessons I'd learned. I'd gone to the States and learned from my host families and friends and now I was being tested. Could I apply those lessons to my life now I was 3,000 miles away from the context in which I'd been taught them? I drew on the advice I'd been given, and my previous experiences, to adapt to life in Boulazac.

STEPPING OUT OF MY COMFORT ZONE

Boulazac is a village, and everyone goes to the games. It was a big deal for them, which added pressure. At first I hated it. This was my first taste of what it feels like to be completely out of your comfort zone. I wasn't with people like me. Even when I was around people, I was kind of trapped in my own head because I couldn't get the language down. This was a big test.

But it was a quiet space and I started to wonder whether I'd made the right call by going there – had I listened to my intuition or had I listened to people around me? Some people had been saying, 'Look, you have a certain amount of time to play and then your career is over. It's about making money.' That wasn't my natural position, but I felt the pressure to earn. College sport is amateur – you don't get paid – so that's five years of your life without making any real money. The Americans were saying you have to make as much money as you can, as quickly as you can. As were my mum and dad, who were encouraging me to plan for a nice little set-up later. But chasing the money had put me in this alien environment.

I was stuck again, thinking what is the right thing to do? What's important for me? When I started I wanted to play in the NBA because it's the best; I moved to Bethel High School because it was the best – it wasn't because it was pretty or glamorous. That's why I was willing to stay on the bench for a year – I wanted to do it because it was important to put myself in competition with the best. It made me happy. Going to France was always meant to be a stepping stone to get back to the NBA.

CONFRONTING YOUR COMFORT ZONE

When was the last time you stepped out of your comfort zone? What was the driving force behind this and what did you get out of it?

_____

_____

_____

_____

_____

_____

_____

_____

_____

_____

_____

_____

_____

_____

_____

_____

DOPE LESSON

Above all else, back yourself

You are going to find yourself in positions like I was in France, in a new environment, with challenges coming at you from several angles. It can be overwhelming, and the temptation is to back down and begin to play a role that makes other people feel comfortable. To get back in the box. In my experience, that only leads to one place: your unhappiness. If you cannot be you in an environment, it isn't the right one for you. Always back yourself and see where it leads – you'll be surprised. The universe seems to reward those who persistently turn up in all weather and are true to themselves and their compass. Keep going and things will happen for you.

THANK YOU, FRED

There was one French guy who was looking after me: Frédéric Adjiwanou. He taught me a few of the basics about being a pro and took me under his wing. He was married to an American and had gone to school in the States, so we'd been on similar paths. That got me through that hard year. Even though it wasn't easy, I managed to get back into the rhythm and finished strong. You need to be able to put things in perspective, and Fred helped me do that.

Most of the team were French, plus one American and one Nigerian – all much older than I was. I learned that I'd been in that situation before, where I hadn't backed myself or trusted my intuition or the lessons I'd learned before. It was hard, but I had to trust that there would eventually be an upswing. I had to go with my gut instinct, that inner compass.

IT WAS
HARD, BUT
I HAD TO
TRUST THAT
THERE
WOULD
EVENTUALLY
BE AN
UPSWING.

After that year, I had two offers from French teams, and other second division teams. Porto in Portugal was also offering good money. But then I got an offer from a Greek team, Aries Trikalla – it was a team in the first division but they were offering me almost half of what I made in my first year. I just wanted to prove what I was capable of. I'd gone to France as a stepping stone; it was harder than I thought, but I stuck with it and now I had a decision to make: money with Porto or a higher level of play with this Greek team. I thought about it, trusted my gut, stayed true to my values and went after the level. I said yes to Greece.

The money was bad, but it was a case of putting my money where my mouth was. It wasn't as easy as just quitting school and maybe sleeping on a couch like it had been a few years ago; this was now my livelihood. I believed that I was good enough to play at a higher level, so now I had to prove it. It was a big call though – if I fluffed this one I would have been in a very difficult situation. Mum and Dad had got to a point now where they had to trust me because I'd called it correctly before, so they were more supportive. My agent understood it, the strategic element made sense – if I had carried on in the second division, that's the level I would always be seen as. So, I trusted my intuition and made sure everything lined up.

Sometimes, we play down our talents and dreams to match others' expectations of us, or limit our achievements to fit the box that society has put us in – we can start to believe that is who we are. It's key to follow your gut in these situations, to take a leap of faith and trust yourself and your gut. This intuition will not lead you towards anything destructive. In the short term, this leap of faith may not make much sense to those around you but, in long term, the fruits of your faith and labours will become clear.

DOPE LESSON

Perspective is crucial

Having Fred – that one ally – made such a huge difference during that first year in France. Having him to speak to about things, and dipping into my past experiences, helped me have the confidence to make the decision about Greece. Maybe without that I'd have chosen the money, but having that foundation helped me see the situation clearly and go with my instinct.

GET ON YOUR BIKE

I didn't have a lot of money when I arrived in Greece. I didn't have a car. I was cycling into practice and into the town centre. I was in a one-bedroom apartment with my girlfriend at the time. It was humbling, but it was the right place for me; it's where I needed to be in order to figure out who I was. The season started off quite well: I'd had a really good game and it felt like Pittsburgh, where I'd backed myself and it paid off. Things were going well; my inner compass was being rewarded. But the next game, I was four minutes in and I pulled my hamstring. Bang! I was out for two months.

DOPE LESSON

You will be tested

As soon as I got injured I thought, is everyone right? Have I made a terrible choice? The people around me had those 'I told you so' expressions on their faces. I was backed against a wall and one thing I know is that we become our true selves in those situations. In relationships it's in the hottest arguments where the deep truths come out. It's human nature. You can't fake instincts. That's why, when people are in difficult positions, they all of a sudden start making decisions fast, and they revert to their true selves because they're backed into a corner. A lot of people can break at that point. It's not something you can explain or validate with those around you; it's an internal challenge. I was in that corner and I had no choice but to let my compass take over.

HAPPINESS IN A RECESSION

I knew I was going to come back. I was young, hungry and I wanted to make my mark. The injury was serious; two months is a long time to be out with a hamstring injury, and the doctor said that if I'd injured it more severely it could have been career-ending. But I was lucky; I'd chosen Greece because of the level I could play at, but the people were incredible as well. They were so warm, not just the coaching staff but the townsfolk too. It was a hard time because I was there in 2014, in the middle of a huge recession that was tearing the country apart. It was serious; to give you an example of the way it affected life, there was a limit on how much you could take out of the cash machines because the banks were scared people would withdraw all their savings.

HAPPINESS COMES FROM DIFFERENT PLACES,

DEPENDING ON YOUR INDIVIDUAL SITUATION.

Despite the situation, the people in this little village were so positive. They didn't have that much, but they loved life. They lived full lives. They didn't have huge cars, but they were really warm and content. You'd see groups of older people meet up at the coffee shop, just chatting and making jokes. They were always smiling. I thought, what's their secret? It was an eye-opener. They didn't need a white Mercedes or a massive fridge full of Gatorade – **happiness comes from different places, depending on your individual situation.** We can find genuine happiness in different ways; it's hard to comprehend it because that is not what you are taught. In the West it's always presented that a 'simple way of life' is something that weirdo hippies do. I'm a product of the western world; I'm from London and I lived a quarter of my life in America, but I've seen more happiness in those small Greek villages than in any other place I've lived.

DOPE LESSON

Never stop learning

You're supposed to be privileged, but you don't have the freedom to be who you are. We all need to realise that we don't have to feel guilty about being ourselves. Every single one of us is born unique via their DNA: no two people are the same. Knowing we are all different, how can we all be happy if we conform to a strict set of rules? You lose this sense of individuality over time, after being told for years and years to conform. We can have similar abilities, we can be a community, but we all have our own path that we need to be brave enough to follow. I started to think like this in Greece. This was another chance to learn – school never stops. It was another chance to pick up a new way of thinking.

MY OLD FRIEND

I remember seeing an old man in the village who lived a very simple life. He was retired and spent his time going to pick up his grandchildren from school and talking to his friends in the coffee shop. We would talk now and then and he'd say to me, 'Can you not see how happy the people are here?' This was a country that was facing its worst crisis since the Second World War, and he pointed out that you rarely saw unhappy people there. That hit hard and made me open my eyes. Yes, I had financial goals, but I knew that wasn't where my happiness lay.

I came back slowly from the injury. My coach was anxious. He was a funny guy; he'd be screaming and seem angry, but in reality he was really just asking for a coffee. When I first arrived there it was intimidating because the interactions that the Greek lads would have with each other seemed super-intense from the outside, but really they'd just be having a laugh.

The coach wanted me to come back for what they call a 'tune up' game, because the game after was a must-win. But I was confident I would be fine, and that we would win. We just missed out on the playoffs, but I came back and finished off strongly. It was one of the best years of my career and it was also the year in which I made the least amount of money, which – I think – speaks for itself. The next year I went on to earn almost four times what I'd made in that season in Greece. But the money was really not important; it was the experience I'd gained to get there that was truly of value to me.

DOPE LESSON

Materialism isn't the one

You can have all that money but it doesn't guarantee anything. It's a cliché, but I think that happens because so many people are following a compass set by other people. It's so easy to ignore your own instincts. It's hard as well because if you get to that so-called promised land, where you have wealth and prosperity but you're still not happy – how do you speak out about that? You're trapped because everyone around you is saying you've got it all, but in reality you are struggling. That was the secret to the old Greek guy's happiness: he wasn't interested in material wealth.

VIVA ESPAÑA

My next move was to UCAM Murcia in Spain. I knew I had to go, as Spain has the best league in Europe, the biggest league after the NBA – again, I was going after growth. Madrid, Barcelona, Valencia – the big dogs were there. It was a shot at the top. I was really focused; I went in there and was locked in. This was another very important stepping stone on my journey trying to get back to the States. I started hot, and I felt confident after the Greece year and coming back from a period of adversity. I played in a pre-season tournament and the general manager at UCAM got in touch with my agent, Pedro, to say he was impressed.

At the beginning of the season, I felt like I didn't get the opportunity to play my best, to prove myself and my worth to the team. But I waited and continued to work hard. I couldn't lose track of my end goal. I knew I would get my chance – I just needed to be ready.

THE KEY TO HAPPINESS

Make a list of your emotional goals, rather than material ones.

_____

_____

_____

_____

_____

_____

_____

_____

_____

_____

_____

_____

_____

_____

_____

_____

_____

We came back from a game on the road in Tenerife and we practised as soon as we landed, so there was pressure to pick up the performance. That practice I landed on my ankle and I knew it was a bad one. I was rushed back after three weeks because I was needed for a big game, but then I turned my ankle again in practice. It was really bad this time, and I was in a tough spot.

I didn't let it get me down. I'd been injured before, I knew I could come back. That put a lot of things into perspective for me. I came back later in the season and played a game. Things still weren't right so I called it quits for the year and began to focus on the year after. It was a serious injury – I'd damaged two of the three ligaments on the outside of my ankle, so they had to operate on it to strengthen it and allow it to heal.

DOPE LESSON

The right move might be the hardest

In basketball, and in life, hurdles will present themselves: you're getting prepared for something big and disaster hits; you don't get that job you went for; your relationship doesn't work out the way you thought it would. Sometimes all you can do is stay prepared and focus on returning stronger. It can happen repeatedly as well. You recover from one down moment and then bang! Another one hits you. It's at times like that you need to turn to friends and family – those who have your back.

CAN'T GO OUT LIKE THAT

The next season my whole deal was, how can I bounce back? I remember speaking to my mum at the start of that season and telling her, 'I don't know if I can trust my body to move the way I want it to.' It was hard; I'd never felt like that, but this was the second big injury in a few years. Pre-season was rough; I hadn't played in a while and I wasn't as sharp as I could have been. The fans who had been supportive the previous season were now saying in the press that I should be sacked because I wasn't up to scratch. They would whistle when I had the ball, and that was very tough. It affected me; I became unsure of myself and began playing timidly. I was playing the role that the fans gave me – a useless player who wasn't as good as he should have been. I was working hard after practice to improve but I was scared to play. I didn't want to shoot.

One of my teammates, an American called Clevin Hannah, pulled me to one side after a game where I'd played really badly. He said to me, 'I know you've got more in there.' He was telling me that I couldn't go out with that attitude. 'You can let people say whatever they want to say about you, but you can't go out like no bitch.' When he said that, something in my mind just snapped. **If you're going down, you've got to go down swinging.** Show some fighting spirit. I'd worked so hard to get here and now things were falling apart and I felt powerless to do anything. That conversation made me realise I could take control. He was right: I'm not going to go down by acting like someone I'm not; if I'm not happy or doing well I'd rather go down while being myself.

The next game, I played my best of the season. That was just before the national team break and I had Clevin's words ringing in my ears, screaming at me – whatever happens I'm going to be myself. By any means necessary I will do things my way. Clevin and I still laugh about that conversation to this day. It was some necessary realness from a true friend.

DOPE LESSON

Who is in your corner?

In life, you need someone close to you who can spot when you're wavering, who tells you to take the risk. Even if you know it's the right thing to do, sometimes you need a prod. In Boulazac that help and support had come from Fred; in Virginia it was Coach Huck and Dom. Sometimes you need someone who will jump with you, or at least encourage you. Without that it can be very hard to do.

Take a look at your friends – how ambitious are they? Are they complaining about their jobs? Are they unhappy with their day-to-day relationships? If you don't want to have a clichéd relationship – look at your friends again. Are they cheating on their partners? Do you want to be around that? Ultimately, it's the influence of the people around you that makes the difference – if you don't surround yourself with good people, who is going to be there to make sure that you make good, right decisions?

Make a list of the people around you who you know you can trust and rely on.

1

2

3

4

5

6

7

8

I WAS A WARRIOR AND I'D BOUNCED BACK

BOUNCEBACKABILITY

First game back after the break, it was like an explosion. I went on an amazing run of games and everything just flipped. The coach was saying, leave the other Ovie in London, forget about that guy. Me and Clevin would be laughing about it. Whatever you do... don't go out like no bitch. It was wild because at the beginning of the season the fans were down on me, and by the end I was a fan favourite. Some of the fans would write to me and tell me that I was one of them now, that I was a warrior and I'd bounced back.

I made the all-star team, and we got to the final four – the semi-finals. We played against the Greek team AEK in the semis and it was insane. We met in their stadium and the atmosphere was incredible. The crowd was going ballistic from the first minute. I played well but we lost ultimately. Despite the disappointment, it was for experiences like that that I'd come to the team in the first place. It was one of my best basketball memories and it felt like I'd come a long way from being that boy who bounced a ball under a bus on Great Cambridge Road. I've had so many different experiences that have proven the need to follow your gut and your instinct. It is about being who you are; your intuition is to be trusted above all else. Nothing else can speak to you that loudly – in my opinion it's there to help you survive and thrive. But it's so easy to ignore that side of you and push it aside. **You can't achieve dopeness without listening to your intuition and nurturing it.**

LESSONS FROM BASKETBALL

1 **You have to work as a team to win** – Even within your own dopeness, you need teammates to help you achieve your full potential. Those are the people who can push you and offer you the right kind of competitiveness that drives you to a higher level. I had fantastic teammates in the US and back in Europe who helped me grow as a person.

2 **Everyone can be a superstar in their role** – I loved the Chicago Bulls growing up, and on that team you had great players like Scottie Pippen and Michael Jordan, but Dennis Rodman was many people's favourite. He wasn't glamorous or flashy as a player; he did the ugly work and got it done by any means necessary. But it was the way he did it that made him admired. You don't need to be the stereotypical star to become one – with dopeness you can turn even the most unfashionable position into something special.

3 **Learn from any situation** – Being truly dope means being adaptable. You need to adjust and spot the potential to learn in any situation. You might get shouted at by a coach and get so angry that you can't see there's a lesson to be learned. When you can process information and see how the situation – regardless of how intense it might be – can be a positive one, you'll learn to trust your inner compass and take the good while disposing of the bad.

HOW TO SURVIVE DARK PERIODS

I've had plenty of tough moments while playing basketball. The lows can seem like they might go on forever. What I've found is that by following these steps, it's possible to rationalise your feelings, organise them so you know which ones to embrace and which to ignore and, above all, create a plan to navigate your way out of those tough moments.

1 **Think in cycles** – Life is cyclical: it has ups and downs. Dopeness will not envelop every moment. You can be the richest person alive but there will be good days and there will be bad ones. The key is to acknowledge and understand that you are going along for the ride whether you want to or not. When you're in a low part of the cycle, you need to realise that it is a necessary part of your journey. It allows you to reach the highs.

2 **Remember the roots** – Most plants need strong roots to survive. They burrow down into the ground and provide the ballast and stability for a tree to grow above the surface. Think of your dark moments like that: they are a way to build resilience. It's hard, dirty work, but you are extending your roots down to make yourself stronger and more secure.

3 **Support systems** – When things do go wrong we all need support. Even in France, when I was isolated, I had that one friend who I could turn to. It helped me get that perspective I needed. Everyone can benefit from that support system. Talk to your friends and family; don't be afraid to reach out – true friends will understand and listen. They don't necessarily need to have all the answers; just having that one person to listen to you and help you come to your own conclusion is vital.

4 **Change your mindset** – Once you've had that conversation with a friend, think about how you can change your own view of a situation. Is there an angle you'd not considered? Is there another way to look at things? Negatives can seem like positives, where there were barriers there can be opportunities. Start by making a list of positives and go from there. Even in our darkest moments we have reasons to be thankful.

SECTION

3

LOVE

MY OWN
EXPERIENCES
IN LOVE HAVE HAD
MANY UPS
AND DOWNS.

I think understanding love and relationships is a key part of dopeness. Having someone to share your life with is dope. All those dope moments seem even better; there's a closeness that is unlike anything else. My own experiences in love have had many ups and downs, so I've picked three key relationships and laid out the lessons I learned from them.

My first love was a big deal for me. As for many people, it was a bittersweet relationship of innocence and experience, as my ideas of what I thought love meant met the reality. You're naive, unguarded. You trust. You don't think things can fall apart because they never have before, not like the way they do when you're in love. It's like stepping into a boxing ring. The first time you're hurt from it you have no defences up, so you take a direct hit. You don't understand it, it takes you by surprise and it's a very new pain. A lot of times with new experiences, if they are bad we won't try them again. It's like food – if you taste something for the first time and hate it, then you're going to avoid that cuisine again; you will be hesitant despite other people who love that type of food advocating for it. You'll remain wary because you remember the disappointment from the first time around.

Because of my first experience with love and the impact it had on me, I've had to consciously take down defences and walls that were not there originally, but which I built because of that first battle. That first negative experience of love, where your innocence is lost, can throw your compass off. That can be detrimental because now you're out there and only seeing a relationship through the lens of a bad experience in the past. It stops you from seeing the positive things about your first love or other romantic encounters. Everything becomes a negative and now you run the risk of not being able to reap the rewards and benefits of having an open and loving relationship, which can be a very beautiful thing.

Love is serious.

TABITHA

Tabitha was my first love. It was very innocent, open-hearted, the first time I'd fallen into that world of emotions. I was 12 years old. I'd just arrived at school in Mill Hill, and as soon as we met we got on straight away. She had a strong personality, she was very pretty and very smart and was not bothered about me being a popular guy in school. She didn't shy away from giving me her honest opinion, which I liked. It is rare to come across people who have a mind of their own at 12. Tabitha was confident and grounded.

She was the little sister of one of my older brother's best mates. So before I met her my brother had told me I was 'going to meet Aaron's little sister, innit'. So I was prepared, or so I thought. The first time I met Tabitha was when I went for the entrance exam. As soon as I saw her I got butterflies. I remember she was giggling and laughing and I thought she was gorgeous. I had to do the exam and all the revision I'd done flew out of my head. I could not stop thinking about her and kept trying to glance over to see her while the exam was happening. After the exam I mustered up the courage to speak to her. I asked her if she was Aaron's sister and she said 'yes' and asked me if I was Raymond's brother. I walked away thinking 'yes, I nailed it'.

I didn't see Tabitha again until I started school, and this time I knew I wanted to get her number. She gave it to me and I wrote it down in my little diary. I went home, looked at the number, picked up the phone, put the phone back down again, and finally steeled myself to actually dial her number and speak to her. The phone was an old-school one, attached to the wall with a cord, so I had no privacy, and I had to speak while sitting on the stairs. But I did it, and we spoke, and I found it easy to open up with her. She saw through the fact I was popular; she couldn't care less about that.

She didn't seem to be overly concerned about the direction of the crowd and that was one of the things I found most attractive about her – her ability to effortlessly follow her own compass. You can always recognise someone who is following their own compass – they've got something special. Your insecurities will make you want to push them away, or your inner compass will draw you closer. In this case, I experienced the latter. I was mesmerised by this person who stood out and seemed to genuinely think for herself, at an age where, quite frankly, there is so much change going on with your mind and your body that it's difficult to know in what direction your inner compass is trying to guide you.

THE TEXT THAT CHANGED EVERYTHING

Later in the year there was a ski trip, which I couldn't go on. That trip really showed up the dividing line in my school between those who had money and those who didn't. I went over to my cousin's house that weekend and I remember getting a text from Tabitha while she was on this trip, saying, 'It's not working, I want to go in another direction.' The text hit hard, it was like a big plot twist in a romantic drama.

I remember feeling happy at first that she was texting me, and then, as it dawned on me that she was breaking up with me, I just fell silent. It was such a sharp pain. I was confused, I was shocked, I was angry and upset. There were so many different emotions that hit me at once. It was the first major rejection in my life and I didn't have any defences up. When you're not expecting anything like that, the pain feels even worse. So I didn't quite know what was happening. I could feel my whole inner compass changing within me. Over the next couple of weeks I experienced a change; that same person who had given me confidence and made me feel on top of the world was the same person who made me angry and bitter. I was embarrassed.

I was trying to put up a front and didn't want to show how much I'd been hurt. When I got the text I was shattered. When I first read the message my vision went blurry, I was so seriously affected by it. My cousin saw my body language change from positive to negative; he asked me what was wrong and I couldn't even say anything. I showed him the text. He told me it was going to be alright and tried to be there for me. With guys it is hard, though, because when boys are young they're not taught to get in touch with their emotional side. The extent of the support was 'you will be alright'.

Now the defences were up, I wasn't going to be vulnerable again; **there was no way I was going to be caught out by love again.** No way. I was with Tabitha on and off for around four years. We got back together but it was never quite the same. I wouldn't allow myself to get to that vulnerable place – that highest part of the mountain that you have to be able to take off all the baggage to get to. Those heights are only attainable if there's nothing blocking the way, if you are fully committed, and I was not willing to do that again.

We broke up initially, then got back together, and I internalised the pain. I was different then and I was young. I was never going to be a sucker again. I didn't want to be open with her and risk her throwing that back in my face. As my basketball developed I had the chance to go to America, and I asked her if she wanted me to stay. She said no, which was a big deal to me. She knew I wanted to go and she knew how much basketball meant to me. I didn't realise it at the time, but that first romantic experience changed my attitude towards love a lot. As a kid I thought you just have a wife, a couple of kids and then that's it. A dream vision. But I hadn't anticipated the trust aspect – how much you have to open yourself up, with the risk that it could all crash and burn.

YOU HAVE TO OPEN TO OPEN YOURSELF UP,

WITH THE RISK THAT IT COULD ALL CRASH AND BURN.

DOPE LESSONS FROM MY FIRST RELATIONSHIP

1. TALK

I didn't talk to my parents about how I was feeling because I thought they would brush it off; same with my brother – he'd just think it was little kid stuff. I can't emphasise enough how important it is to voice how you're feeling. You need to be able to talk to people about issues like this. If it's real to you, it will be real to them. In the back of my head I was scared that on top of the rejection I'd suffered, people close to me might have not taken it seriously. But that is a risk worth taking. Those conversations can help to give you a fresh perspective. Choose who you confide in wisely, you might be better off talking to a friend or a cousin, but do reach out because even the act of sharing removes some of the burden you've been carrying around internally.

2. RISK AND REWARD

Up until my first experience with love, I thought relationships were straightforward. You find someone you like, settle down, job done. But after Tabitha I learned that there is always risk and reward. You've always got to put something on the table in order to receive. There is always something at stake. Without that you'll be so uncommitted that any reward won't be satisfying. After Tabitha, I no longer cared about the reward because I was too concerned with being hurt. I said to myself, I do not want to have pain, I don't care if I don't get all the beautiful things that come with a loving relationship – I just don't want to be hurt again. It took years to get away from that, and it's something that, if I'm honest, I still work on to this day.

3. YOU CAN'T ALWAYS GET WHAT YOU WANT

My experience with Tabitha taught me that even if you think things are working out, there can be influences outside your control that send things off course. That's not your fault. You can't blame yourself. After things broke down between us I started to blame myself. The biggest struggle for me was separating that failure with my own personality. Wasn't it proof that me being myself and going in my own direction was in fact the thing that possibly chased off the first person I ever loved? I feel like this is a very easy trap to fall into for many of us. When we're vulnerable it's very easy to confuse others' acceptance of us for our value.

4. DON'T QUESTION YOUR OWN DOPENESS

You can dwell on love and the good or bad experiences that come with it, but don't let the bad ones push you to questioning your own dopeness. Learn and grow from each experience and hold on to the good things. This might be painful at times, but it's important not to deprive yourself of the joys, and the power that is only truly accessible through love. Even more importantly, never validate the love you have for yourself through the love someone else may or may not have for you.

REBECCA

I met Rebecca on my first day at Bethel when I went for a visit to look around. I was walking up and down the hallways between lessons. She just smiled at me and those fluttering butterflies appeared again. I asked the guy I was with, 'Who was that?' He asked me if I liked her and made an introduction. 'This is Ovie. He's from London. London, England!' I stood there looking and sounding stupid. I remember being nervous but I managed to get her number. We texted over the summer before school started, so I felt like I got to know her properly. She was raised very well – she was very respectful, funny, bubbly, and a bit shy. She had a fun, outgoing side to her, but she had to take a liking to you for you to see it. We got close really quickly: we would go to church together; she was a cheerleader and would be at all of my games.

HAVE YOU EVER HAD YOUR HEART BROKEN?

How did it make you feel and what have you learned from it since?

_____

_____

_____

_____

_____

_____

_____

_____

_____

_____

_____

_____

_____

_____

Everything was going awesome, and I knew it had got to the point where she really, really liked me. When she told me how much she liked me, I knew what that meant: if she's opening up to me then that means I'm going to have to open up to her. Then that shaky internal compass started twitching and the fears and worries began to present themselves. Those old scars started to throb again. That old pain resurfaced. 'Don't you dare go down that road' warning signs are going off... Not that love shit again.

Inside I knew that Rebecca was a good girl for me. She could be a long-term thing. But I wasn't ready to put myself out there again. When I told Rebecca I wanted to break it off, it was as brutal and random as what Tabitha had done to me. I'll never forget her coming to my house after practice that day and she stood in the rain outside the front of Dom's house asking me to change my mind. My guard was up, so I was only able to empathise up to a certain point – I'd shut myself off. It was an awful feeling, but that's how powerful that initial pain had been. I didn't even want to admit that I'd been the one to make her upset, but I had. After that day, once she left, we never spoke again. That set off a cycle for me.

MORE LESSONS IN LOVE

1. BUILDING A WALL

When I got to America my walls were up. I went further than that even. I built a moat, the drawbridge was up, there were crocodiles in the water and a guy on a speed boat with a gun. I was still sociable and getting on with everyone, but if you made it to the moat you weren't going any further. I wasn't going to risk that again. But allowing people we care for into that interior world is how your relationship begins to grow; it's where those bonds are formed. They can't be created externally – you've got to be able to open up. That comes down to trust in yourself and that other person.

2. YOU'VE GOT TO CONNECT

With Rebecca, she opened up to me. She had such a gentle and genuinely caring soul. But because of the walls that I had built up, my fear did not allow for my heart to connect. I wanted to, but that would have meant me being in a vulnerable place again, and I wasn't ready for that. The fear of taking another hit is real and so we find ourselves rejecting connections with really amazing people. Without openness and true connection, the foundations of any relationship won't be solid. You have got to connect.

GINA

After more fruitless relationships, I told myself that I had to take a risk if I was going to get close to anyone else again. I'd moved to Pittsburgh, I'd changed teams, I'd changed perspective in terms of the way I was approaching basketball, so I felt I needed to do the same in my love life.

I knew that the first time around with Tabitha I had no reservations or fears, so I could take the plunge without even knowing I was doing it. What I realised is that you have to take that risk every single time you go into a romantic situation. If you're into someone and you're both at a place where you know things could develop into something special, you have to risk something – **you have to take a leap of faith.** Without being able to do that I was just leaving a trail of destruction in my wake. I'd been in winning situations and managed to mess it up because I didn't want to roll the dice. I was too scared of being hurt.

That wasn't because I did not want something real or of true substance, I really did. It was the walls and protective barriers I put up, that had originally kept me safe, that over time began to hold my heart hostage. **This inability to emotionally connect past a certain point was starting to make me isolated** and question if that first special encounter that everyone has with love was a fluke.

BREAKING WALLS

What walls have you built up around yourself to protect yourself from getting hurt?

_____

_____

_____

_____

_____

_____

_____

Now, what can you do to break down these walls?

_____

_____

_____

_____

_____

_____

_____

_____

_____

YOU HAVE TO TAKE A LEAP OF FAITH

In Pittsburgh I met this girl Gina. I decided I was going to risk it with her. I knew I could not keep getting into this cycle of drawing people close and then pulling up the drawbridge as soon as they wanted to get inside. It wasn't good for them and it wasn't good for me. We'd been talking for a while and I was being completely honest, completely faithful, and completely straight up. But the fact that it was a long-distance thing – she was still living in Virginia – put a strain on the relationship from the start. I couldn't put my finger on where the arguments were coming from. She'd get annoyed if I wasn't constantly in touch with her; it was trivial and petty stuff. I couldn't figure out how to stop it.

We ended up sitting down and I asked her, 'Where is this coming from? Why are we like this? Is there something you want to discuss?' But we still didn't get to the root of what was happening. That lasted for about eight months and we tried to salvage it a few times, but again I'd put myself out there, and again it blew up. Maybe I wasn't ready because I wasn't really dealing with the huge amount of insecurities that still surrounded my love life.

This monster has followed me around. I've not fully managed to shake it off and I know that behind it is where the rewards are. I could not get fully invested in these relationships. You know when you're giving it everything and putting yourself on the line, and I just wasn't. I wanted what Dom's parents had. These relationship woes made me appreciate what they had so much. They let each other be vulnerable and trusting.

After Gina, I was alone for a while. I didn't want to keep on being halfway invested in relationships. It took its toll on me because I started to think: 'Can I connect with anyone? Am I just this isolated person who isn't willing to let his guard down? What is wrong with me?' You've put so many barriers up that you've forgotten how to connect. **We're here to give love to our families, to our friends and partners. When we're not able to do that, it torments and eats away at us.** I was alone for a while, deliberately, but now I'm trying to be more open. I don't want to pull up my drawbridge again, but letting someone in is still hard. Like I said at the start of this section: love is not easy.

LOVE LESSONS I'VE LEARNED

1. THE SHUTTERS MUST COME UP

It took me a while to realise how much that initial experience of rejection changed me. Then it took time for me to realise I needed to work on my reaction to it. I do know now where the areas for growth are for me and that I need to work on myself. I've seen love, I've had it and I know it is out there, but for a while I convinced myself it wasn't worth the risk. To get to this point I had to put my guard up, but to move forward that drawbridge must be opened. You have to take a chance.

2. SACRIFICE SOMETHING

You get to a stage in life where you can do as well as you want, but there comes a point where you have to give in order to receive. In order to keep on growing you need to sacrifice something. It's the only thing that can give you a sense of fulfilment. It's impossible to live this life and get to a certain level without giving something back – all successful people do it. In love this is true as well. Be willing to risk something, to sacrifice something. It's only by doing this that you will get something in return.

3. PAIN ISN'T ALWAYS A BAD THING

Understanding that pain and negative feelings are a part of love is vital. It's like going to the gym and realising that if you wake up the next day and you're sore it's because you're actually growing – you've put in the good work. It might hurt in the short term but ultimately it's worth it. In any truly dope relationship, your partner will push you. They will ask for those extra reps you might not want to do, but it's those difficult moments that can lead to the most growth.

4. EMBRACE VULNERABILITY

Everyone who has had good or bad experiences of love has one thing in common: we were all vulnerable. At some point we didn't have our defences up, and that allowed us into a place of happiness. Try to think back to an experience of love that was satisfying. At one point in that

THIS INABILITY TO EMOTIONALLY CONNECT CONNECT PAST A CERTAIN POINT WAS STARTING TO MAKE ME ISOLATED.

relationship, you felt a happiness that was so pure at times, it resembled a dream. But that level of happiness only came because you allowed that person to see your weaknesses and flaws. That made you feel like you did not have to 'fit in' around them. That kind of vulnerability in love allows for our true self to blossom, and it is the hardest thing to do.

5. TAKE ON A CHALLENGE

I challenge you to be courageous, to allow your compass, your true self, to have a chance at love; you will be surprised where love and a well-set compass will take you in this life. Take chances, be vulnerable, and allow someone to love who you are, because YOU ARE DOPE.

***

REMEMBER: YOU CAN CHANGE

Lately I've come to a greater realisation. This might sound strange, but I've come to grips with my own mortality – I'm not going to be around for ever. I want to experience some of the finer things, and love is the finest thing that you can have on this planet.

I was trying to fill gaps with things that took the place of love, but I realised that would never satisfy me. It was never going to fulfil me in the same way. You can't buy a car or a house or a pair of trainers and think that they'll replace love. We're here for a finite amount of time, so we need to grasp that and bear it in mind. I think that's something people learn as they get older – they care less about what other people think because they realise it's superficial and not that important. Maybe that's what the old Greek guy was getting at.

I'm not trying to make love sound easy, because it isn't. But you won't get to your destination without pulling down that drawbridge and allowing someone in. Like me, you might waste a few opportunities before you discover this, but I'd recommend trying to avoid that – the hurt you can cause is real, and long-lasting too.

For me, I wanted to start living life on my own terms. That includes my love life. What use is listening to your inner compass about other life decisions and then ignoring it when it comes to those key romantic relationships? I know about the mental walls that I've built in my brain. I know what triggers my defences to go up, and instead of giving in to those instincts I've started to manage them. You have to think about why those sirens are going off and learn to cope with them. Once you've done that, you can start to trust your potential partner and ultimately make the most of your own potential.

It doesn't matter how many times you've been hurt, you can take control. You can change and embrace dopeness in your next relationship. You don't have to keep making the same mistakes. The key is to stop, take stock and see where you're going wrong, instead of getting stuck in a loop.

OPENING UP

When was the last time you allowed someone to see your weaknesses and flaws?

_____

_____

_____

_____

_____

_____

_____

_____

_____

_____

_____

_____

_____

_____

_____

_____

DOPE LOVE TIPS

1. BE OPEN

Try not to let the past colour your future relationships. People deserve a fair chance. If your compass is wavering it might be out of fear of what came before. It's natural. But don't prejudge someone's motives – give them a chance to get to know you and what you're really like.

2. BE TRUTHFUL

It's OK not to be interested in someone. But be honest. Don't be with someone because it's convenient, or easy. Everyone deserves the chance to find true dopeness in love and if you are only halfway committed, that's fake and ultimately doomed to failure.

3. BE INTRIGUED

If you can't wait to find out more about someone, about what makes them tick, you're onto something. That inquisitiveness is what fuels relationships. It also allows you to open up. By asking questions you start to peel back the protective layers that people wrap themselves up in.

4. BE AWARE

Know what triggers send up your shutters. Is it someone asking those penetrating questions? If so, tell them. Let them know about your past experiences. They've probably had them too. If you get anxious about someone being distant or stand-offish, again confront it. You don't have to be over the top – just probe to see if this is someone who isn't interested or is just bad at communicating.

5. BE YOURSELF

Throughout this book I've spoken about my own battle with conformity and how it didn't chime with who I am. Ultimately what I learned is, it is OK to be yourself. Being different is a good thing and this extends to your love life too. When you find someone who accepts you for who you are, it's unlike anything else. That is true dopeness. No one should settle for anything less.

SECTION

4

HOW
DO YOU
ACHIEVE
DOPENESS?

REAL LIFE
DOESN'T
HAVE
A FILTER,

THE SOCIAL
MEDIA WORLD
IS NOT REAL.

You've read all about me, my life and my quest for dopeness. You've seen the challenges I've faced and how by conforming, by getting boxed in and not listening to my inner compass, I've been knocked off course but eventually found my way back. I bounced back by deciding to be myself, and to dedicate time to working on my dopeness.

In this final section I want to give you some bite-sized guidance on how to focus on your own dopeness.

SOCIAL MEDIA: SOURCE OF DOPENESS? NOT NECESSARILY

Our lives on social media are the lives we want to have and the lives we want to show. It's not real life. It's a manicured, honed, picture-perfect representation of a life. You need to know that before you pick up that smartphone and start browsing through these carefully designed accounts. Everything is considered, from the way a picture is cropped to make it look idyllic, to the exact time the posts are put online. It's like a huge video game and the goal is desire.

Think about who you are following and why. Consider that word: follower. This is an age of following. We're all looking for disciples, people who have bought into us as online personalities – whether that's friends, family or often complete strangers. Andy Warhol once said that in the future we'll all be famous for 15 minutes. There was no form of social media when he was revolutionising the art world in the 1960s, but he was right, and social media is the method for delivering that fame.

But just remember real life doesn't have a filter, the social media world is not real. That's vital to bear in mind because if we allow that line to be blurred, it can set off a negative chain of events that will ultimately prevent you from attaining your own inherent, freely available dopeness.

Once you know how dope you are as an individual, that can protect you from some of the more negative aspects of social media. That herd mentality I talked about is rooted in social media. It's what it depends on and feeds on. If you can make hundreds of thousands of people believe a certain thing is desirable, some of them will buy it. If you can appear to have all the answers and supply that in a steady stream of videos that just happen to feature ads promoting certain brands, people will buy into you.

It's not all negative – people can be guided in a positive way, but if we let the unreal world of social media be the ideal we are aiming for, or comparing ourselves with, we'll never be happy. I'll let you into another secret: you're never going to be as happy as some of the people you follow on social media. Why? Because that world simply does not exist. It's a façade. It is an advert for a life that is – for the vast majority of people – only attainable in tiny chunks.

You can get it if you holiday in that one spot where the pictures look just right. You can get it if you rent that car and pose in front of it in the right way. But what is that? You can end up tailoring your life to fit in with a lifestyle you're not able to live and that you're copying directly from social media. Is that following your inner compass? Or are you being manipulated?

Think about how many celebrities have come forward to talk about their negative experiences of fame? How many of them talk about the pressure to appear perfect, to never make a mistake, to project 24/7 an idea of who they are rather than the actual person they were destined to be. For most of us, we don't have that pressure – we can live our lives without that kind of intense scrutiny. I personally think we should be thankful because our inner compass is easier to tune in to. We don't have the background noise to contend with. **If we're able to drown out the buzz of social media, and the peer pressure that comes with it, we'll have a clearer path to our own dopeness.**

RESHAPE THE RELATIONSHIP

I'm not saying we need to throw our smart phones in the bin and go live off-grid in the mountains, but now and again it's so important to switch off from the online world. You're doing it now while reading this book, and those little pauses in our screen time can make all the difference. Should life be seen as a never-ending competition? Where we constantly measure ourselves up against our friends and ultimately ask: who is doing better? Is that healthy? Should that competition then be amplified online? No, I don't think so. Yes, let's use social media for the positives it brings: great connectivity with people all over the world and a platform to spread our messages and to receive them, but always remember to question what you are getting out of it and, most importantly, what you are putting in? What are you giving away? Remind yourself, it's a product like any other and it's always selling something to you. Here's a simple way to test whether you're getting something out of social media or not: is the thing you're looking at on your screen in any way contributing to your dopeness? If not, think about spending your time on something that will.

The second you're not enjoying social media my advice is to get off it. Delete the apps from your smartphone. Have a break. Are you happier? Much happier? Then maybe you don't need it in your life. You can be hurt by it emotionally and mentally because it's stressful to try to keep up with. It can lead to negative self-thoughts, where you convince yourself you can't do something before you've even started. 'Oh, I can't do that.' 'That will never work.' 'You're not good enough.' As a wise person once said, **the key to life is mostly just showing up.** By putting yourself in positions to try, and sometimes fail, you at least have the chance to win. If you don't succeed that time, maybe you'll learn a vital lesson that will make you bounce back stronger; perhaps you'll readjust and pick another path you weren't expecting. It's always better to try and to risk failure than not to try at all because of the fear of what other people might think.

MY EXPERIENCES WITH SOCIAL MEDIA

I have been media trained since I was in high school in the US. Image is so important for sports teams over there that we were told how to behave online in order to protect ourselves and the sports programmes we were part of. That was a part of our media training, so I've had a certain code of online conduct drilled into me in the same way that I was taught how to screen or hit a fade-away jump shot. In fact, in high school we weren't even allowed to have Twitter, as it was seen as too much of a liability where one misstep could result in some outrage or scandal that would embarrass us and the school. I've got to say, looking back, that was a smart move. How many young sports people have you seen mess up on Twitter, Snapchat or some other social media site and then have to apologise and in some cases perhaps lose contracts or have their reputation tarnished. It happens all the time and is simply part of life.

You probably won't have that scrutiny, but it's still important to think about how you act. We're encouraged to have an opinion about everything these days, with mouthy TV personalities giving their 'take' on everything, most of them designed to elicit a response which is usually outrage. Say something controversial and watch the views on YouTube roll in as millions of angry people hate-watch your 'take' or nod along approvingly if it reflects their own opinion. I'd say form your own views but consider this: sharing them on social media might not be dope. Unless you know what you're talking about, why is that going online? Is that dope? Or just straight up stupid? In the immortal words of the Breakfast Club DJs: don't play yourself.

CAUTIOUSLY BEING MYSELF

I had to be cautious and careful because whatever the public sees on social media has to line up. The image has to be correct. As a basketball player you have your professional self, the athlete, the sportsman, but

SHOULD LIFE BE SEEN AS A NEVER-ENDING COMPETITION?

there's also the person behind that. The real me. You are two completely different people. Ovie, the athlete or Ovie, the guy off the TV, and then Ovie, who goes home and looks forward to a plate of jollof lovingly prepared by his mum.

When people fall in love with you, they love the athlete – people love Michael Jordan, the basketball player. They don't love Michael Jordan the man because, in all honesty, when have they seen him? They saw the guy flying through the air and redefining basketball, but is that the same guy who goes home to North Carolina and sits in his mum's house? Nah, I don't think so. Same for any big sports star like Cristiano Ronaldo or Serena Williams, the fans don't love the person – they love the icon.

When I went on *Love Island* **I had the chance to be the Ovie that my friends and family always saw**, not the basketball player who was told to stay off social media and be risk averse. In the villa, that was me, 100%. After I left the house, social media became a big part of how I stayed in touch with fans. It was a way for me to interact and be myself while communicating with millions of people. I use it as a way to show who I am and be positive. It's a platform for me to help spread a positive message because I think anyone who gets that kind of fame or exposure should give something back and help people. I believe you can only give when you have something. On social media I try to dish out dopeness, and you can only do that if you have dopeness to give in the first place.

DOPE LESSON
FOR SOCIAL MEDIA

The half rule

The half rule is simple. Calculate how much time you spend on social media. Take that number and divide it in two. Now spend half of that time off social media and working on yourself. We live in the attention economy, where our eyeballs are what companies want and social media is the most potent way to get our attention. But figuring out how much time you spend on social media will:

1. PROBABLY SHOCK YOU

2. GIVE YOU MORE TIME FOR YOURSELF

Try to use it to do some of the things I suggest in this book. Make a list of five things you want to achieve in the short term, medium term and long term. Make a gratitude list of all the things you are thankful for. Use the time to check in on friends or family and really ask them how they're doing. Maybe you'll realise you don't need social media – it needs you.

Be honest with yourself, how much time do you spend on social media each week?

_____

_____

_____

_____

_____

_____

_____

_____

Now list all the other things that you could have achieved in that same amount of time.

_____

_____

_____

_____

_____

_____

_____

A LESSON FROM LOVE ISLAND

The biggest thing that stuck out for me once I left *Love Island* was how much people reacted to me being different. That was the thing they embraced. It wasn't the clothes (although they were sick), it wasn't the fact I was a basketball player, it was the fact I went on to this reality TV show and acted like myself. People loved it. They responded to being given something that was out of the ordinary.

It proved that you don't need to stick to what is popular or what's trendy. **You can be yourself and thrive.** By sticking to who you are and your own dopeness, it will attract the right people. The lesson I learned from secondary school, when I realised not being myself was potentially hugely negative, was proved right. People were constantly telling me how they loved the fact I was different and that I didn't conform. Naturally, not everyone felt that way, but more than enough people did to make me realise I'd made the right choice at 16 to change my path.

I was overwhelmed when I came out of the house because of the love that people showed me. I was stunned. I felt like I'd just been in my house for a couple of weeks, then gone outside and suddenly everyone in the world seemed to love me. It made me want to tell everyone that their uniqueness is special too. People seemed to be able to relate to me because, I believe, they know that they're different too. They want to be able to develop their own dopeness. That's what this book is all about. A roadmap to your own dopeness, with stops along my journey to show you what I've learned.

Fans of the show seemed to love that I was able to show emotion, that I was revealing a softer side of myself and treating it as completely normal. We're not used to seeing that from men and that's something that needs to change. It's unnatural to push that aside. It's normal to be different. It's strange to try and conform and do what we're told because everyone else is doing it, not because it's where our hearts lie.

My experience is proof of that on a large scale that everyone can see.

WHEN YOU LOSE TOUCH WITH WHO YOU ARE, YOU BEGIN TO SABOTAGE YOURSELF.

DON'T LISTEN TO DOUBT

As we all know it's very rarely the doubters that stop us from embracing ourselves and becoming our better selves. It's those who are closer to us who make those throwaway passing comments which can sting the most. It's the joke that your mum or dad says which unknowingly can cut straight through your confidence and make you question the vision you had inside yourself that said, 'You're different, you're dope.' In my story I had to overcome those jokes and negative energies that can trap us within ourselves, and it's so important to be able to overcome these challenges. And hopefully in this book I've shown you how.

When you lose touch with who you are, you begin to sabotage yourself. When you play into conformity, you subconsciously try to undermine your choices. You ignore your intuition when it becomes drowned out by judgemental voices. This is the dilemma that a lot of us face today and many of us end up in a rut, with the fear of being different. I argue that as good as it is to acquire knowledge and listen to everyone around you, you need to be guided by that internal compass.

DON'T HIDE WHAT MAKES YOU UNIQUE

I handled being different in a number of ways and I'll tell you about when I was successful and when I wasn't. One way was trying to hide my accent in order to fit in in the US. I would talk with a twang when I was in Virginia. I did it to fit in because I could not be bothered with the million questions that would ensue: 'Oh my God, where are you from? Are you from France? Do you speak French? Are you from London, Engerrrrlund. So you speak French?' They were being serious too. People genuinely asked me that question with a straight face.

During my time in Pittsburgh I decided to drop the twang entirely. I was bored of it. Overnight I turned into a mini celebrity on campus.

People were like, hey, there's this tall black guy and he's from London, really from London. People really love people who are different. In the locker room the guys would take the piss, asking if I would have tea with the Queen. But they were really intrigued. And I knew that, so I would be able to laugh it off. It's something that you have that they don't.

They took the piss, but really, I should have taken it as a form of flattery – they just wanted to be able to share their own differences too. **People try to hide their own insecurities by pointing in the opposite direction** – so they point at you, the different one. Every time someone does this to you, you just have to know that they're doing it because of their own insecurities. When I decided to talk in my normal accent it was nuts. Teachers loved me, I got on with everyone on campus, even the ladies who worked in the university restaurants loved me and gave me extra food. 'Here comes London!' they would shout.

There was just so much love and it blew my mind, and was sort of like a nail in the coffin of my insecurities and self-doubt. I thought, it's OK to be yourself, don't mind the whispers and get past the turbulence. As long as your mind can push you to your own lane and really embrace that path, the world will love you for it. It might take them time but they will come around. That was one of the first times I really felt comfortable in my own skin as a young adult.

I think the weird thing was people not questioning why a guy from London was talking with a twang. Why were people not taking the piss out of that? It's because it made them feel comfortable, in my opinion. It makes people feel comfortable when you conform to what they're doing. Because then it doesn't make them think about who they are. The more people don't have to pay attention to the internal battle that they're facing, the more they can ignore the compass inside themselves. If everyone acts the same as each other, you all become confirmation that it's OK to be a part of the herd. It's constant validation. But the second someone steps away from the herd and stops giving you the validation of conformity, it makes you think about yourself and your own issues.

All over the world everyone conforms to cultural norms, but in America that following-the-herd mentality is strong. And it was funny because opportunities opened up for me because of my accent. I ended up going to a private brunch with the Pittsburgh Steelers NFL team when I was in uni, with the great and good of Pittsburgh society, judges and politicians. That happened because I met a news presenter who had come down to the arena to watch a basketball game. It was during my year on the sidelines but I'd gone down to watch the game and we got talking on the baseline. He was shocked that someone from London was out here in Pittsburgh, took my number and invited me to the gathering.

If he thought I was another kid from Pittsburgh, he probably wouldn't have done that. He was just intrigued by the difference. That's the thing – most people that are part of the herd will be intimidated by difference, but those people who are in powerful positions, they're intrigued by it. They're secure in what they're doing. They are drawn to difference. They're able to spot someone who has tuned that inner compass. They think: 'He's got a boat that's going somewhere', and no one wants to be part of a crew or be on a boat that has no destination. People are ultimately drawn to those who have a clear direction and who believe in themselves. Changing my accent was a simple step. **It was me being confident in being me, in embracing my inner dopeness.** But I didn't always make the right call.

During my first year as a professional player in France, I couldn't speak the language. That ended up making me feel isolated, which was hard but also gave me a lot of quiet time to consider and be at ease with the fact I was different. The next year I moved to Greece, where I was happy to be on my own. I was proud of my difference and it gave me confidence on and off the court. I was in a unique situation with a group of friends who were all so different from each other – yet we all embraced each others' differences. But when I went to Spain I almost fell into the trap of conforming, which left me feeling frustrated. My story is not straightforward, like most people's it zigs and zags, but hopefully you can take something out of it that will inspire your own dopeness.

THE DOPENESS SNOWBALL

It's helpful to think of your own dopeness as a snowball that starts off as something you can fit and mould in the palm of your hand. There's not much, but there's a tangible amount to start with. Once you start to build up a bit more dopeness, you can put it on the ground and roll it. If you're on your path, that snowball will start to grow, collecting more snow – or in this metaphor, dopeness – along the way. Once that path is in front of you, the goal is to keep pushing. There might be obstacles. They might even stop you or knock you off the path, but if you can stop, take stock and refer back to your guide – your inner compass – you can make the adjustments to get back on track. Then it's a case of pushing again, and you'd be surprised at how much easier it gets when you're on that right path.

Sometimes you don't even feel like you're pushing – you're just going along with the flow, building up this huge snowball of dopeness, of experiences and advice that you can fall back on when your route to dopeness is tested again. And trust me, it will be tested. It's not like you keep moving forward and get to a certain point in your life and that's it, no more struggles. Life fluctuates. There aren't any straight lines. Some people have things made easier for them because of their socio-economic background, or the class group they belong to, or the status of their parents who can help guide them down clearer paths, but even those privileged people need to find their inner compass – even they can end up down the wrong path.

BUILDING YOUR OWN HOUSE OF DOPENESS

When you get into that dark corner, my advice is to sit down and take out a pencil or a pen and a piece of paper and list everything that you're thankful for. Just make a note and have a think about the blessings we

HAVE A THINK
ABOUT THE BLESSINGS
WE HAVE, BECAUSE
IT'S THAT
PERSPECTIVE
THAT CAN HELP
YOU RECHARGE.

COUNT YOUR BLESSINGS

Make a list of all the blessings in your life right now.

_____

_____

_____

_____

_____

_____

_____

_____

_____

_____

_____

_____

_____

_____

_____

have, because it's that perspective that can help you recharge, take stock and face the challenges that you might have convinced yourself were too difficult. Be thankful for the air that we breathe, for waking up every day, for our families, for all those things we take for granted.

The more of these things we can be thankful for, the more 'wins' we have before we face day-to-day life. If we can be truly thankful and humble, it creates a solid foundation to build on. **You can construct a house of dopeness which is always there to fall back on when you face a loss or are in doubt.** When social media knocks you off track, that piece of paper can be your reference – your textbook for resetting and getting that sense of perspective.

It's hard to be fulfilled without that house of dopeness, especially when social media has us striving for something that is, as I said earlier, impossible to truly attain. You can follow the trends, buy the designer suit and a flashy car, but is that fulfilling? Not in my experience. I've been in that situation before when despite being blessed in so many ways, I was unhappy as a result of constant comparison. Why don't I have that car? Why don't I have that house? When I was alone in France as a first-year pro I'd look around and want what my peers had. But when I started to get the better contracts and material possessions, I was still unhappy and that made me stop and think.

You can get into a pattern where you're not thankful for anything you do have and simultaneously be discontent at everything you don't have. It's impossible to be happy when you're in that trap. So tread carefully and remember your reasons to be thankful. Start with the smallest things and keep them close at hand, either mentally, or maybe as a note on your phone for easy access, whenever those pangs of envy or unhappiness start to creep in.

KEEP IT TIGHT

I have my close-knit friends and family. I have four close friends who I hang around with, and if I'm not with them I'm with my family. My friendship group is tight and made up of people who I knew before I went to America. If you're surrounding yourself with social media or people who you're not comfortable being yourself with, it's easy to lose touch of your true motivations.

It's important to have those friends who know you and have seen you change. That means they're better placed to flag up if you're going off track – if you're not acting like yourself or if you're trying to fit in rather than be yourself. With my friends I don't feel the need to be different. I'm allowed to be myself, 100%. There's no expectation for me to be someone other than who I am.

BE SELECTIVE

For me it's a real process to make true, real friends. Friendship shouldn't be something that is given out lightly. You've got to know this is someone who understands and accepts you for who you truly are. They need to value you, and you them, an equal amount. There's a partnership there. They play a crucial role in you feeling confident enough to be who you are. If you're acting in unnatural ways to please them, that's when things can start to go awry.

CHECKING IN WITH FRIENDS

Since experiencing a reality TV environment, I see even more of my close mates now. To be dope, you've got to be a good friend. I check in on them: how are they feeling; have they got any big life events coming up that are stressing them out; is their inner compass locked in on what they want out of life? That's a crucial part of being a dope friend. Just turning up and asking a basic set of questions where you'll be able to tell if someone is struggling or not.

WHEN YOU'RE TRYING TO WALK YOUR OWN PATH IT'S OFTEN SCARY

You feel like you're chopping your way through the undergrowth with a machete and sometimes there are snakes and wild animals waiting for you. The friendship you offer can help reassure someone that they are taking the right steps, that going down this untrodden path is actually the right thing to do, regardless of how hard it is. It's easy to take the wrong road because it's easier, but you need to be there to let your friends know being dope can only be achieved when you take the harder path. You can give them that little boost they need to get them over the line and – most importantly – let them know that they are not by themselves. They have support.

ROLE PLAYING ISN'T COMPATIBLE WITH DOPENESS

One thing I learned playing basketball is that adopting a role can destroy your own dopeness. As you learn a role that's been assigned to you, it's easy to regress. By accepting the limitations imposed on you, shutters go up in your brain and they push back against you. You don't even realise it until it's too late. By that point you're already not as confident as you should be. You're no longer certain of yourself and your actions. This happened to me and it threw off my basketball trajectory.

When I got to college, I had a couple of knocks, and then all of a sudden you're asking yourself: do I want to fit in and not ruffle feathers or do I want to be strong? Being different puts people's backs up. They have to confront the fact someone is coming in and doing things in a new way. I faced pushback against that and had to ask myself if fitting in was more important than me saying no, I'm going to do things my own way, even if that makes me an outsider.

I conformed to the group and that meant I put a shade over my light in order to fit in. By doing that you can get into a rut.

At work, the more you conform, the more you get used to fitting in to the larger group because you don't want to ruffle feathers. That's cool because you've made them happy by not highlighting their insecurities, but by doing it you're putting a huge cap on your potential. You can lose sense of who you are because now you're not being you – now you're playing a role.

When I first got to the States I was super aggressive: if I thought I could do something I would do it, if I wanted to go for something I would do it – there wasn't any hesitation. But as time went by I changed my position to conform. I changed position to help out the team, I stopped working on certain skills and areas so that I could focus on what made other people happy.

It's important to help others, but you shouldn't lose yourself in doing so. That's a trap that a lot of us can fall into. The more you conform, the less you work on yourself. Call it self-care, if you like. The longer you play the role of someone else, the more you lose your skill set and lose what makes you, you. If you're playing a role, that's all anyone else will ever see. We need to nurture our differences and work on ourselves – that is truly dope.

THE MOST
FULFILLING
THINGS IN LIFE
OFTEN COME AFTER
NAVIGATING THE
HARDEST ROUTES.

YOU ARE DOPE

Remember when I told you the story of the basketball rolling under the bus? I mentioned that because we are all human and make mistakes. As humans, we are surrounded by lots of voices, especially when we are young, that tell us to conform and be the same as everyone else. We're told to toe the line. Some of that advice is right; it's invaluable and we can only see it with the advantage of hindsight.

But one thing that you need to remember is that, whether you fit in with others easily, or you stand out from the crowd, you are dope. There is no fun in trying to complete a puzzle when you already have all the answers. The most fulfilling things in life often come after navigating the hardest routes and making mistakes along the way. This is the thing that I think stops a lot of us from following our hearts in a direction that will lead us to true happiness. It's easy to get caught up in the moment, but it's the ongoing journey of life that we'll learn the most from.

I'm speaking from experience. When I decided that I was going to get a scholarship to go and play basketball in the States, I didn't know the first thing about how to make it happen. That wasn't my concern. I knew if I followed my heart it would be the driving force to do whatever was necessary to satisfy my real desires. We see our parents do it all the time – it's what pushes them to the limits in order to give their children what they want. So why don't you? Why don't you trust your heart? **Don't drown out the sound of what your heart is telling you: amplify it instead.**

SO, WHAT ARE YOU WAITING FOR?

Write down everything that makes you **DOPE** and, most importantly, **OWN IT**.

1

2

3

4

5

ACKNOWLEDGEMENTS

First and foremost, I would like to thank the man upstairs – God. I am not a perfect Christian, but my faith has played a huge role in my journey. It is something that cannot be explained but something I have felt has been a source of strength, comfort and encouragement at some of my lowest points. I have always appreciated how far hard work can take you, but along the way, regardless of how hard you work, we all need to catch a break, and for this I thank God.

Secondly, I would like to thank my mum Foluso Soko, my dad Raymond Soko Sr, and my older brother Raymond Soko Jr. My immediate family have not only played a pivotal role in me becoming who I am today, but they have also always been a source of love and motivation for me in my down times as well as the smooth times. I think it takes a lot for a family to allow their youngest to leave and follow their dreams at such a young age, and from such a distance. I think it took a lot of trust and a huge leap of faith and courage to allow me to travel halfway across the world to chase the dream of being a professional athlete before really knowing if I was any good at it. For that I will always be grateful.

Last but not least, I would also like to give thanks to the Cowell family. This was the family that welcomed me into their home and loved me like a brother and a son. Clayton Cowell Sr, Linda Cowell, Dominique Cowell, Kim Kerns and Gloria Barbour. Thank you, guys, for taking me into your home, caring for me and mentoring me during such important years of my adolescence.

There have been many people who have had an impact on me, played a huge role in my journey, and from whom I have gained so many life lessons. These are the life lessons that I am sharing with you guys. Without the impact of every person that I've encountered along my journey, I would not be the person I am today.

Thank you.